SOVIET MILITARY TRENDS:
IMPLICATIONS FOR U.S. SECURITY

WILLIAM R. KINTNER
ROBERT L. PFALTZGRAFF, JR.

AMERICAN ENTERPRISE
INSTITUTE
1200 17th Street, N.W.
Washington, D. C. 20036

FOREIGN POLICY
RESEARCH INSTITUTE
3508 Market Street
Philadelphia, Pa. 19104

William R. Kintner is the director of the Foreign Policy Research Institute and a professor of political science, University of Pennsylvania.

Robert L. Pfaltzgraff, Jr., is the deputy director of the Foreign Policy Research Institute and an associate professor of international politics, The Fletcher School of Law and Diplomacy, Tufts University.

Special Analysis Number 6, June 1971

Second printing July 1971, third printing March 1972

Price: $3.00

Library of Congress Catalog No. 71-170291

Contents

The authors, as well as the American Enterprise Institute and the Foreign Policy Research Institute, are indebted to the persons below for their counsel and support.

Theodore C. Achilles
Vice Chairman, Atlantic Council

Murray Baron
Murray Baron Associates

Joseph A. Beirne
President, Communications
  Workers of America

C. H. Bonesteel, III
General, U.S. Army (Retired)

Francis Boyer
Director, Smith Kline & French

D. Tennant Bryan
Chairman of the Board
Media General, Inc.

W. W. Keen Butcher
Butcher & Sherrerd

George Champion
President, Economic Development
  Board of New York

Peter B. Clark
President and publisher,
The Evening News Association

W. P. Clements
Chairman of the Board
SEDCO. Inc.

John H. Colburn
Editor and publisher,
The Wichita Eagle

Robert Dechert, Esq.
Partner, Dechert, Price & Rhoads

Elbridge Durbrow
Director, Freedom Studies Center

John M. Fluke
President, John M. Fluke Mfg.Co.

Kenneth W. Gemmill, Esq.
Partner, Dechert, Price & Rhoads

Mills E. Godwin, Jr.
Attorney, Suffolk, Virginia

Edmund A. Gullion
Dean, The Fletcher School of Law
  and Diplomacy
Tufts University

Loy W. Henderson
Professor of Foreign Relations,
American University

Foy D. Kohler
Professor, Center for Advanced
  International Studies
University of Miami

Paul Laxalt
Attorney, Carson City, Nevada

Morris I. Leibman, Esq.
Partner, Leibman, Williams,
  Bennett, Baird & Minow

L. L. Lemnitzer
General, U.S. Army (Retired)

W. L. Lindholm
Executive Vice President
American Telephone & Telegraph Co.

Neil McElroy
Chairman of the Board
The Procter & Gamble Company

Robert E. McNair
Partner, McNair, Conduras &
  Corley
Columbia, South Carolina

Wilfred J. McNeil
Admiral, U.S. Navy (Retired)

Covey T. Oliver
Professor of Law
University of Pennsylvania

Lewis Powell, Esq.
Partner, Hunton, Williams, Gay,
  Powell & Gibson

C. Brewster Rhoads, Esq.
Partner, Montgomery, McCracken,
  Walker & Rhoads

Charles E. Saltzman
Partner, Goldman, Sachs & Co.

Richard F. Staar
Associate Director, Hoover Institution
  on War, Revolution and Peace
Stanford University

Philip Van Slyck
Philip Van Slyck Associates

Foreword

This study was initiated early in 1971 as a joint project of the American Enterprise Institute for Public Policy Research and the Foreign Policy Research Institute. Its purpose is to analyze the implications of growing Soviet military capabilities for the security of the United States. The study embodies both a theoretical analysis of alternative Soviet foreign policy emphases and an examination of developing Soviet policies in the major regions of the world.

As part of this project, a conference was held in Philadelphia on February 26 and 27, 1971. The following persons attended, and their contributions, both during the conference and in subsequent comment on the draft manuscript, were invaluable.

Harold Agnew
Director, Los Alamos
   Scientific Laboratory

Vincent Davis
Chester W. Nimitz Professor
   of Social and Political Philosophy
Naval War College

James E. Dougherty
Professor of Political Science
St. Joseph's College

Waldo H. Dubberstein
Professor of International Affairs
National War College

Richard B. Foster
Director, Strategic Studies Center
Stanford Research Institute

William E. Griffith
Professor of Political Science
Massachusetts Institute
   of Technology

Daniel James
Author, foreign correspondent
Resident of Mexico

Morton A. Kaplan
Professor of Political Science
University of Chicago

George Lenczowski
Professor of Political Science
University of California, Berkeley

Charles Burton Marshall
Professor of International Politics
School of Advanced International
   Studies, Johns Hopkins

Norman D. Palmer
Professor of Political Science
University of Pennsylvania

Robert C. Richardson, III
Brig. Gen., U.S. Air Force (Retired)

Frank N. Trager
Director, National Security Program
New York University

Donald Treadgold
Professor of History
University of Washington

Richard L. Walker
Director, Institute for International
  Studies
University of South Carolina

Of the many who assisted in the preparation of this study, we wish to give special recognition to Harvey S. Sicherman of the Foreign Policy Research Institute.

The authors, of course, assume full responsibility for the study's contents.

William R. Kintner
Robert L. Pfaltzgraff, Jr.

Relative Military Capabilities: The United States and the Soviet Union

Introduction

In an interview on March 9, 1971, President Nixon said:

> There are two great powers facing us, Russia and China. . . .
> Certainly neither of them wants war. But both are motivated by a
> philosophy which announces itself as expansionist in character. This
> they will admit themselves. And only the U.S. has sufficient strength to
> be able to help maintain a balance in Europe and other areas that might
> be affected.[1]

The military balance between the United States and one of these powers, the Soviet Union, has changed greatly over the past decade. This study examines the change and analyzes its implications, both for the conduct of Soviet foreign policy and for the political "balances" in various regions of the world. In addition, Soviet approaches to arms control negotiations, international organization and other major global problems will be assessed.

The Nature of the Soviet Military Buildup

The great increase in Soviet strategic and conventional military power relative to the United States is no longer a matter of controversy. Within a two-week period early in 1971, the President of the United States, the Secretary of Defense and the Chairman of the Joint Chiefs of Staff all delineated the existing and projected force levels of the Soviet Union and the United States.[2] (Comparative U.S. and Soviet military forces are presented in Appendix A.)

The most significant elements of the Soviet military buildup relate to strategic forces, naval forces and research and development. With respect to the first of these, President Nixon declared: "We believe the number of Soviet strategic forces now exceeds the level needed for deterrence." [3] More explicitly, he asserted:

> The design and growth of these [Soviet] forces leads inescapably
> to profound questions concerning the threats we will face in the future,

---

[1] Interview with C. L. Sulzberger, *New York Times*, March 10, 1971, p. 14.

[2] *United States Foreign Policy for the 1970's: Building for Peace*, A Report to the Congress by President Richard Nixon, February 25, 1971; hereafter cited as *Building for Peace*. See also *United States Military Posture for FY 1972*, Chairman of the Joint Chiefs of Staff Admiral Thomas H. Moorer, United States Navy; *Statement of Secretary of Defense Melvin R. Laird on the FY 1972-76 Defense Program and the 1972 Defense Budget*, before the House Armed Services Committee, March 9, 1971.

[3] *Building for Peace, op. cit.*, p. 129.

and the adequacy of our current strategic forces to meet the requirements of our security.[4]

As to naval forces, Admiral Thomas H. Moorer summed up as follows:

> The Soviet deep water fleet, over the past decade, has been steadily expanding in size and capability. They are expected to have some 217 operational combat surface ships by the middle of this year, and this number will probably increase through the 1970s. In contrast to our fleet, which still has a sizeable number of combat ships more than 20 years old, the Soviet fleet is much newer, with very few ships more than 20 years old.[5]

With respect to research and engineering, Dr. John Foster, Defense Department Director of Research and Engineering, testified in recent posture hearings before the armed services committees of the House and Senate that, since 1968, the Soviet Union has allocated most of its funding in research, development, testing and engineering to the military.[6] Since 1968, there has been an annual growth rate of about 15 percent in Soviet military expenditures. As a result, the Soviets will be devoting the equivalent of about $11 billion to military R&D during fiscal 1972, 40 to 50 percent more than the United States. Secretary of Defense Laird has acknowledged that "reductions in technological areas already have seriously affected our ability to sustain essential technological leadership." [7] While the Soviet Union forges ahead in the deployment of high payload ICBMs, the United States probably possesses advantages in penetration aids, the MIRV technology and (undeployed) ABM systems. At best, U.S.-Soviet R&D competition "is a horse race, with the U.S. now ahead by a neck, but falling back." [8]

Finally, a supplemental statement to a Report of a Blue Ribbon Defense Panel, submitted to the President and the Secretary of Defense on *The Shifting Balance of Military Power,* September 30, 1970, clearly delineated the end of U.S. superiority and a dramatic shift in the balance of power.[9]

---

[4] *Ibid.*

[5] Moorer, *op,cit.,* pp. 27-28.

[6] Donald C. Winston, "Soviets Sustain Military Research Growth," *Aviation Week and Space Technology,* April 12, 1971, p. 23.

[7] Secretary Laird estimates the Soviet level of R&D spending to be 10 to 12 percent higher than our own. (Laird, *op. cit.,* pp. 37-40.) Although the Department of Defense is asking for an increase of 12 percent in spending ($7.89 billion for fiscal 1972, compared with $7.11 billion for fiscal 1971), the increase will neither make up for the years of relatively lower spending nor match Soviet expenditures.

[8] Dr. John Foster, "The Soviet Threat to U.S. Security," *Air Force,* November 1970, p. 82.

[9] The Blue Ribbon Defense Panel, appointed by the President in July 1969, submitted its report on July 1, 1970. At that time, members of the panel reserved the right to submit supplemental statements on areas not addressed by the panel's report. This supplemental statement, dated September 30, 1970, and signed by seven members of the Blue Ribbon Defense Panel, was not released by the Defense Department until March 12, 1971.

These seven members were: William Blackie, chairman of the board, Caterpillar Tractor Co., Peoria, Illinois; George Champion, president, Economic Development Board of New York; William P. Clements, Jr., president, Southeastern Drilling, Inc., Dallas, Texas; John M. Fluke, president, John Fluke Manufacturing Company, Inc., Seattle, Washington; Hobart D. Lewis, president, Reader's Digest Association, Pleasantville, N.Y.; Admiral Wilfred J. McNeil, director and advisor, Fairchild-Hiller Corp., New York, N.Y.; Lewis F. Powell, Jr., attorney, Richmond, Virginia.

While the relative decline of U.S. strategic power is a matter of fact, the meaning of this development for U.S. security is the object of controversy. Since the approximate destructive power of the Soviet and U.S. strategic forces cancel each other, it is easy to conclude that the political utility of nuclear weapons is greatly diminished, if not eliminated. To base U.S. policy on such a conclusion, however, would ignore the *political* derivatives of modern military capabilities.

When nuclear parity obtains, the state which possesses superior local forces in a region such as Europe or the Middle East cannot be dislodged from its position by the threat of a nuclear strike against it. Thus the advent of nuclear parity has had the political consequence of reducing the role of the U.S. strategic nuclear force as a counterbalance to the superior conventional forces facing our allies in many areas. U.S. alliances and political relations founded upon that linkage are correspondingly weakened. Furthermore, if one examines the nature of the instruments of deterrence possessed by both sides, the very concept of "parity" comes into question.[10]

The capacity to retaliate after a first strike is affected crucially by the type of weapon available. Current American ICBM and Polaris capabilities would be most effective against cities, the so-called soft targets. In contrast, the Soviet nuclear force, with its SS-9 ICBM armed with a 25 megaton warhead, seems to be designed primarily for destroying ICBM silos and other strategic capabilities *without* employing the smaller warhead SS-11 ICBMs or missiles deployed on the submarine force. The United States could retaliate with its Polaris squadrons primarily against Soviet cities. But this would still leave the Soviet Union with a capability for destroying American cities. In these circumstances, as President Nixon has asked:

> Should a President, in the event of a nuclear attack, be left with the single option of ordering the mass destruction of enemy civilians, in the face of the certainty that it would be followed by the mass slaughter of Americans? [11]

If the USSR possesses a counterforce first-strike arsenal, possession of even an assured second-strike capacity by both sides is *not* the equivalent of *parity*. The threat of such a Soviet counterforce capability is precisely the reason for the alarm over the Soviet strategic programs, which emphasize the counterforce SS-9 and the countercity SLBM (Polaris-type). President Nixon described this ominous development in his 1971 "state of the world" message:

> Our deployments of offensive missile launchers were completed by 1967; the USSR continued to build different types of land-based ICBM's and a nuclear-powered missile submarine force that will equal ours within three years at current rates. The USSR has constructed a

---

10 There is no evidence that Soviet strategists recognize parity as a stable condition; in fact the concept is dialectically impossible. At best, parity in the Soviet view connotes a transitional stage between Soviet inferiority to Soviet superiority.

11 *United States Foreign Policy for the 1970's: A New Strategy for Peace*, A Report to the Congress by President Richard Nixon, February 18, 1970, p. 122; hereafter cited as *A New Strategy for Peace*.

large ICBM, the SS-9, for which the U.S. has no counterpart. Deployed in sufficient numbers and armed with the multiple independently targetable warheads (MIRV's) of sufficient accuracy, this missile could threaten our land-based ICBM forces. Our MIRV systems, by contrast, do not have the combination of numbers, accuracy, and warhead yield to pose a threat to the Soviet land-based ICBM force.[12]

The political consequence of this sort of "parity" (which is really U.S. inferiority) is the elimination of the U.S. nuclear force as protection for our allies and friends against a Soviet military incursion, or at least a major decline in its credibility. Doubts are increasing among United States allies. They are asking to what extent would the United States be prepared to invoke strategic nuclear weapons for any purpose short of a direct military threat to its own national territory, if to do so would be to risk its own destruction.

---

[12] *Building for Peace, op. cit.,* pp. 189-90.

Important Considerations

Before discussing the implications of improved Soviet military power for Soviet foreign policy, it is revealing to recall the security dilemmas which President Kennedy faced ten years ago. As reported by James Reston:

> A profound debate is now going on here at the highest levels of the Government over how to keep the Communists from expanding deeper into the weak states along the Communist borders from Korea through Southeast Asia to Iran. . . . Washington, according to General Lyman Lemnitzer [chairman, Joint Chiefs of Staff], has "at the present time the power to destroy the Soviet Union," but is losing in Laos and Cuba and is deeply worried about South Vietnam and Iran.

> According to the argument which is now prevailing in the debate, "the United States must either take on a large financial deficit to provide a more expensive combination of limited war capacity, plus nuclear or massive retaliatory force, plus longer-term foreign aid programs, or risk total nuclear war or a series of piecemeal military and diplomatic defeats." [13]

It is obvious that the United States has lost the trump card of strategic superiority which it possessed in 1961 but still faces problems created by the same adversary in the very areas which bedeviled U.S. policymakers a decade ago.

The Soviet Union, for its part, adheres to a doctrine of historical evolution which can be described only as expansionist—that is, it posits the eventual triumph of the Soviet brand of communism as the future world order. "Its ideology," asserts Milovan Djilas, "has been reduced to a weapon of expansion and authority." [14] Although it is difficult to measure the coincidence of Russian national interests and Marxist-Leninist theories, the theme of the increasing influence of the Soviet Union throughout the world is dominant. As Leonid Brezhnev put it at the 1971 24th Congress of the Communist Party of the Soviet Union:

> In recognition of its international duty, the CPSU will continue to pursue a line in international affairs toward promoting the further activation of the world anti-imperialist struggle and the strengthening of the combat unity of all its participants. The total triumph of socialism the world over is inevitable, [applause], and for this triumph, for the happiness of the working people, we will fight, unsparing of our strength. [applause] [15]

---

13 James Reston, *New York Times,* May 14, 1961, Section 4, p. 10.
14 *New York Times,* April 1, 1971, p. 41.
15 Text broadcast by the Moscow Domestic Service, March 30, 1971, as published in *Daily Report* (Soviet Union), Federal Broadcast Information Service, March 31, 1971, No. 62, Supplement 17.

The nuclear era has forced a considerable revision in Soviet notions of what is acceptable in the cause of advancing communism. Since the mid-1950s, war has no longer been considered inevitable to the ultimate success of Soviet communism. Called "peaceful coexistence," the revision emphasizes a "continuum of conflict," that is, political conflict at a less dangerous level. The Soviet Union favors the revolutionary, national liberation war in which the need for direct Soviet intervention is minimal and hence the risk of escalation that would threaten the Soviet Union is slight. Such warfare, in Soviet theory, is both "just" and safe. Soviet strategy provides both for the early resort to strategic capabilities and for the use of capabilities at other levels of confrontation with an adversary.

Whether or not the "just national liberation war" reflected past Soviet strategic nuclear inferiority (which may change with the balance of power), we can accept as a hypothesis Soviet declaratory statements that their strategic doctrine and force design eschews "parity" or "sufficiency" and seeks "superiority." And we can then examine the consequences of this hypothesis. Unlike many Western strategic thinkers, Soviet theoreticians perceive positive influences deriving from strategic superiority. In his speech to the 24th Congress of the Communist Party of the Soviet Union, Defense Minister A. A. Grechko declared:

> The constant strengthening of the armed forces is an objective necessity for the successful building of socialism and communism, and one which results from the law-governed patterns of social development and from the particular features of the class struggle between capitalism and socialism. The experience of more than 50 years of socialist building in our country has fully confirmed the rightness of the military policy and the practice of armed forces building being firmly pursued by the Communist Party.[16]

The existence of strategic inferiority, let alone a transient nuclear standoff, has not paralyzed or even restrained Soviet political activity, supported by conventional forces under the nuclear umbrella. Under these circumstances, the Soviet leadership focuses upon the "correlation of world forces"—that is, the balance of power in the major regions of the world—in addition to the global power relationship.[17] The expansionist tendency of Soviet theory and practice, however, has always been guided by the caution inherent in any calculation of the "balance of forces." Any dispute between Kremlin "hawks" and "doves" is likely to be more a quarrel over the assessment of this balance than a fundamental conflict as to the goals of foreign policy. Increased military power in a variety of forms affects Soviet perceptions of this balance as well as the particular application of Soviet strategies in a given theater.

The Soviet operational code requires the party leadership to exploit opportu-

---

16 Text reprinted in *Pravda* (Moscow), April 3, 1971. For an earlier, and similar, Soviet assessment of the political importance of strategic capabilities, see Lt. Col. V. M. Bondarenko, "Military-Technical Superiority: The Most Important Factor of the Reliable Defense of the Country," *Communist of the Armed Forces* (September 1966), translated and edited by William R. Kintner and Harriet Fast Scott in *The Nuclear Revolution in Soviet Military Affairs* (Norman, Oklahoma: University of Oklahoma Press, 1968), p. 354.

17 Wynfred Joshua and Stephen P. Gibert, *Arms for the Third World: Soviet Military Aid and Diplomacy* (Baltimore: Johns Hopkins Press, 1969), p. 111.

nities for political advantage. Premature risk-taking, or adventurism, is to be avoided but failure to gain from a favorable situation is a form of "revisionism" or unnecessary accommodation to the West. The "correct" course of action at any given historical phase is derived from the dialectical view of history which assumes an unremitting struggle between the socialist and capitalist camps until the ultimate victory of socialism is assured. The preferred course of action to reach this end is currently called "peaceful coexistence."

Although it is possible to discern a general pattern of Soviet expansion, there is no way of determining in advance the specific nature of Soviet intentions, except perhaps by reviewing past Soviet actions and programs of procurement and deployment. The progressive expansion of Soviet military force across the spectrum of nuclear and conventional formations indicates both an effort to hedge against as many uncertainties as possible and a desire to acquire the benefits of military superiority. Furthermore, the Soviet Union, like the United States, must deal with a set of dynamic strategic interactions. If U.S. policymakers assume that the Soviet leadership wishes to expand only through political conflict and consequently fail to neutralize the Soviet achievement of a first-strike nuclear capability, the Soviets might choose to exploit the possibility of a nuclear option. Conversely, if the United States seals the strategic nuclear door, the Soviets are likely to rely on political expansion supported by conventional naval and military forces.

In addition to the increasing options that a changing strategic balance affords the Soviet Union, there is the general question of the roles of U.S. allies and the unaligned nations in their relationships with the two superpowers. Essentially, two divergent paths are possible. One emphasizes a growing partnership among free world nations, as envisaged in United States foreign policy under the Nixon Doctrine. Many allies are capable of greater efforts in providing for both their own and regional security. Other nations may be prepared to improve their capabilities if they receive adequate assistance from the United States.

The second is based on the assumption that many nations traditionally have looked to the United States for their ultimate security guarantee and have assumed, rightly or wrongly, that U.S. strength was sufficient to deter or to preclude piecemeal military defeats. The U.S. strategy of the early to mid-sixties seemed to foster this approach. The repercussions of the current Indochina war, and the consequent turning inward by a segment of the American people, may reduce the willingness of many nations to participate in any "partnership for peace"—even though these nations may continue to hold a strong emotional allegiance to the objectives behind such a partnership. The Soviet Union can be expected to exert pressures on these nations, with an objective of influencing them to lean towards accommodation, rather than assuming more of the burden of their security.

A key question for the United States in the decade ahead will be the path these nations choose in the context of a changing U.S.-Soviet strategic equation. As Soviet capabilities relative to those of the United States grow, the options available

7

to the Soviet leadership will increase, while ours will narrow. In fact, this changed condition is already evident in the contemporary world: West Berlin, the Middle East, Southeast Asia, the Caribbean and elsewhere—in regions where intentions are necessarily acted out.

During the 1970s the Soviet Union's growing power will continue to intrude primarily into the American security system and into U.S. alliances. Despite any danger China portends for the Soviet Union, and however the Soviet leadership may be preparing for it, it is the international position of the United States which is endangered by emerging Soviet strength. Thus, a related assumption of this study is that during the decade of the seventies, the Soviet Union will pose a far greater threat than China to the United States. In fact, the desire of Peking to deal with Moscow from a position of strength may be one of the causes of conciliatory Chinese symbolic gestures toward the United States such as the visit of the U.S. table tennis team to China in April 1971. The recent thaw in Sino-American relations, however, offers little promise of achieving an early stability in the Southeast Asia and Pacific Basin regions. Although the People's Republic of China is not a global power it seeks to achieve a global role by the inexpensive support of insurgencies and other revolutionary actions.

Some Chinese leaders regard the Soviet Union as a greater threat to Peking than the United States. Despite efforts at diplomatic reconciliation and trade agreements, there are clashes along the Sino-Soviet border and the two countries have conflicting goals in South Asia. Thus, the civil war in Pakistan has revealed the Pakistani alliance with Peking as diametrically opposed to the quasi-alliance the Soviets now have with India. Further, as Chinese nuclear forces expand, the Soviet Union will become increasingly vulnerable to a possible Chinese nuclear threat as well as to possible Chinese migration into the largely empty Siberian territories east of Lake Baikal. The Soviet Union lacks sufficient manpower to populate these territories. It is, therefore, attempting to develop, across the Indian Ocean, an assured maritime route to the Far East which will provide easier access to this area. A Soviet naval presence in the Indian Ocean and Persian Gulf could pose a threat to West European and Japanese oil sources. In addition, the Soviet Union appears to be seeking to flank China by strengthening Moscow's influence in the Pacific Basin and Indian Ocean area [18] and by expanding its strategic strike forces so as to be able to deal with Communist China, *in extremis,* without at the same time weakening its deterrent position vis-à-vis the United States. Apparently, the Soviets are developing an "all horizons" strategic posture. Unless the Soviet leadership can neutralize U.S. capabilities during the decade of the seventies, it may miss the chance to resolve its conflict with Peking. Not only will it fail to establish a new world order with Moscow at the center but it may find itself between the "anvil" of an Atlantic alliance that includes both the United States and an increasingly unified Western Europe, and, to the east, the "hammer" of China.

---

[18] See Appendix B, p. 35, *Indian Ocean and South Asia.* The establishment of a Soviet fighter base in Ceylon at the request of the Ceylonese government supports this thesis. (United Press International, Philadelphia *Inquirer,* April 20, 1971, p. 1.) Ironically, Ceylon was the first recipient of Communist China's foreign aid program.

Alternative Emphases in Soviet Foreign Policy

Because of the operational flexibility and historic continuity of Soviet foreign policy, we prefer here to deal with alternate policy emphases rather than alternative courses of action. For each emphasis, an *assumption* is made as to how the Soviet leadership views the global military balance and an *implication* is proposed as to how this military power may be employed in the service of Soviet foreign policy. (Throughout this discussion the *fact* of increasing Soviet military power remains a constant.) These emphases may succeed one another as international circumstances render the choice of one or another of them appropriate. They are complementary in many respects and depend, as our review of regions of the world will suggest, as much upon the "correlation" of local forces as upon any nuclear balance.[19] Hence, increasing power need not imply increasing belligerency, but it does supply a fresh option for military force if there is nothing to check it.

A Strategy of Opportunity

Trend. Extension of Soviet influence around the world with an expanding local presence in the form of Soviet economic aid and military advisors.

Assumption. The present Soviet estimate of U.S. will and capacity diminishes Soviet fear of confrontation.

Implication. Attempted Soviet replacement of U.S. influence even by means likely to lead to confrontation: rivalry.

Description. The USSR has been extending its influence into many parts of the world concurrently with acquiring an increasingly favorable power posture vis-à-vis the United States. It will pursue its objectives even more aggressively if it perceives a decline in the U.S. willingness to risk a confrontation. In short, the USSR will seek to extract political gains from the changing strategic balance. It will continue to seek decisive military superiority, both de facto and in world opinion, by rigorous pursuit of qualitative and quantitative improvements, and will utilize economic and political strategies to exploit advantages thus gained to extend influence to regions of the world from which historically the USSR has been excluded.

Consistent with this policy emphasis, Soviet leaders, confident about their weaponry, R&D and long-term viability, would decide that the United States is unwilling to sustain countervailing expenditures and commitments over the long

---

[19] The implications of changed Soviet military capabilities for regions of the world are examined in Appendix B.

run. Through Soviet strategic psychological operations, encouragement would be given to dissidence, anti-establishment propaganda, and disarmament movements. Americans would be encouraged to demand a unilateral rejection of high-cost weaponry as being unnecessary to defend the United States. The Soviet Union would thus take advantage of disillusionment over the cost and outcome of fighting wars of national liberation, the spread of values detrimental to national security among American youth and a growing preoccupation with environmental problems, combined with worsening problems within the American economic system— all of which tend to reinforce trends toward isolationism and anti-militarism in the United States.

The Soviet government would assume that in the 1970s the United States is likely to take extreme steps to avoid confrontation. For example, it would assume that the U.S. will hesitate to resist increasingly bold Soviet actions in areas such as the Middle East. Thus, the Soviet Union would be able to proceed in many areas, its local military option being uncontested. In this framework, the Soviet leadership would conclude that in any nuclear confrontation the United States will favor diplomatic concessions. Hence, the implication of this assumption for Soviet foreign policy is the political exploitation of expanding Soviet military power in order to replace U.S. influence whenever possible, even if this entails likely confrontation. We call this Soviet policy "the strategy of opportunity" because its distinguishing feature is the confidence with which the Soviet Union would exploit its military advantage in support of political objectives. According to this concept, the Soviet Union need have no intention of carrying confrontation to the point of actual military action. In fact, it would be likely that its intention would be to avoid superpower hostilities under all circumstances. But confrontation is not a one-shot tactic. It is a process the length and the number of whose stages depend on how cleverly it is directed. The longer a confrontation lasts, the more likely that a democratic political system will gravitate toward concessions rather than provoke war against a power perceived as being strategically superior.

A Strategy of Caution

Trend. Same.

Assumption. The present Soviet estimate of U.S. will and capacity sustains Soviet fear of confrontation.

Implication. Attempted Soviet replacement of U.S. influence short of means likely to lead to confrontation: rivalry.

Description. This Soviet foreign policy emphasis assumes U.S. willingness to contest Soviet maneuvers, even by means likely to lead to confrontation. Therefore, in the 1970s the Soviet Union will follow a more forward but still cautious strategy against the United States. This more forward strategy will be limited, however, by the desire to avoid a Sino-Soviet military clash leaving the United States the primary beneficiary.

Given this view, the Soviet government would proceed with various forms of political activity and display its "flag" prestigiously, but would shrink from employing military means where confrontation with the United States may result. Specifically, it would seek to avoid employing its military forces in either Europe or Latin America because it is both unsure of its advantage and fairly certain that the United States will resist even if nuclear confrontation should ensue. Thus, the implication of this assumption is Soviet refusal to allow rivalry with the United States to threaten what the United States considers its vital interests because the military balance is uncertain and U.S. resistance predictable. We call this Soviet policy emphasis "caution." According to this concept, the Soviet leadership—for reasons rooted not only in Communist strategic doctrine but also in the Russian historic experience—might at times be even more cautious than the "objective balance of forces" would seem to require. To a certain extent, such a Soviet policy emphasis might arise from a fear that American political leadership is "irrational" and prepared to exhibit, in times of crisis, greater political will than available military capabilities warrant, or willing to commit the United States to a more costly and dangerous course of action than the stakes of a situation would justify in Soviet eyes.

A Strategy of Condominium

Trend. Same.

Assumption. Estimate of U.S. will and capacity sustains Soviet fear of confrontation.

Implication. Movement toward a less conflictive relationship and a compromise with the United States in certain areas. Attempted sharing of influence with the United States as likely to diminish the chance of confrontation, in other words, a situation of partnership.

Description. The last policy emphasis explores a different implication which runs to the heart of the dispute over the "expansionist" or "defensive" nature of Soviet foreign policy. In this scheme, Soviet achievement of nuclear "parity" and the general growth of military power supply the communist government with the necessary confidence for negotiation. This course rests on the assumption that Soviet leaders, having achieved a position of psychological as well as strategic equality with the United States, would become less truculent and would be inclined to resolve outstanding U.S.-Soviet issues so as to preserve traditional Russian national interests.

Thus the Soviet Union would seek a halt in strategic armaments and pursue limited rather than global foreign policy goals. This hypothesis gains some plausibility from the thought that the Soviet Union—located between the Germans, the Japanese, and the Chinese—might at some future time feel compelled, under a new generation of leaders, to cooperate with the United States to preserve international equilibrium and their own security. Domestic constraints, including economic performance and resource allocation decisions designed to placate internal dissent, would perhaps provide additional motivations for such a policy. The

11

Strategic Arms Limitation Talks (SALT), the Middle East negotiations, and European security proposals could be seen as being symbolic of the Soviet desire to end rivalry where such rivalry engenders the fear of confrontation. Under this policy the Soviet Union would favor nuclear strategic stabilization. From this could issue a condominium, characterized by shared influence and responsibility for security in all areas where U.S. and Soviet interests and unsettled local conditions contribute to dangerous situations. Given current U.S. alliances and the geography of the opposing blocs, condominium would permit extension of Soviet influence into many areas formerly protected exclusively by American power and policy. The "partnership" and "strength" aspects of the Nixon Doctrine accord with this model: "negotiation" could provide the formula through which the Soviet-U.S. condominium would be developed. The condominium case derives from the psychological confidence engendered by military equality which, to Soviet leaders, argues for "sharing" global responsibility and influence. The emphasis is less on rivalry than on common interests. In this model, some Soviet policymakers could become apprehensive over too rapid a U.S. disengagement from Europe and Asia.

Conclusion

The Soviet Union has begun to follow the strategy of opportunity increasingly, particularly in the Middle East and the Indian Ocean areas. Although the strategy of caution is currently being employed in Europe, the Far East and Latin America, we can anticipate trends toward opportunity in these regions also. Although we have posited condominium as a logical alternative to Soviet expansionism, it is unlikely that the Soviets are committed to this choice other than as a transitory tactic.

Regional Applications

There is no way of being certain which of the foregoing policy emphases will prove dominant throughout the coming decade. Even as the Soviet Union achieves what its policymaking elites deem to be a margin of military superiority over the United States, one could probably expect to find these elites somewhat divided with respect to preferred strategies. At any given time, Soviet foreign policy may reflect a fluctuating mix of all three emphases described above—opportunity, caution and condominium. In fact, considerable advantage can be derived from playing the three themes simultaneously, the better to control strategic responses of a democratic political system with the characteristics that exist in the United States. Functional cooperation (in such areas as arms control negotiations, scientific space ventures and cultural exchange programs) might very well run parallel with controlled conflict in specific geographic regions (Berlin, Korea, Southeast Asia, the Middle East and the Caribbean). In the meantime, the Soviet Union can be expected to continue developing the total spectrum of capabilities at its disposal in order to broaden the range of options available.[20]

In Europe, for example, the most immediate effect of the Soviet Union's increased military strength is the weakening of the link between U.S. strategic power and West European defense and the consequent reduction of the credibility of NATO's strategy of flexible response. This development has contributed to rising West European interest in a political settlement with the Soviet Union. *Ostpolitik,* pursued by the West German government, represents an effort to improve relations between West Germany and the Soviet Union. Specifically, *Ostpolitik* has consisted of a series of bilateral efforts—between West Germany and the Soviet Union, as well as between Bonn and various East Central European communist states. In the German-Soviet treaty of August 1970, the Federal Republic accepted the postwar Eastern frontiers although ratification of the treaty by the German government was made contingent upon the resolution of East-West differences concerning the status of Berlin.

From the Soviet perspective, *Ostpolitik,* the Moscow-Bonn treaty of August 1970, and the idea of a conference on European security may be seen as quasi-legal devices for gaining recognition of a permanent Soviet sphere of influence and simultaneously encouraging the isolation of the German Federal Republic and the weakening of NATO.

The West Germans, who see themselves as both the object of contention and

---

[20] A more detailed examination of potential implications of increasing Soviet military power for Soviet foreign policy in major regions of the world can be found in Appendix B.

the occupants of the potential battlefield, may increasingly feel that some sort of settlement on the issues of reunification and security can be made with the Soviet Union only while NATO still stands. This sentiment is being exploited by the Soviet government. Since the West Germans are now the financial heart of the continent and since the European Common Market is now proceeding to the last stages of economic integration, *Ostpolitik* can furnish a convenient lever for Moscow to effect a slowing of European political integration.

In the highly explosive Middle East, the Soviet Union is capitalizing on an opportunity strategy, which appears to be cautious because both the local balance of forces and the nuclear stalemate make it possible to create the *fear* of confrontation while avoiding a clearly offensive posture.

As a strategic bridge linking Europe, Asia and Africa, the Middle East has long been a traditional object of Russian and Soviet diplomacy. Recently, the region's great oil reserves, its impoverished population, its political rivalries and religious disputes, complicated above all by the Arab-Israeli conflict, have provided opportunity for maneuver. Soviet support of some Arab states, especially the United Arab Republic,[21] has made those states militarily dependent upon Moscow. As apparent protector of the Pan-Arab policies centered in Cairo, the Soviet government reaps advantages which are denied to Western powers (especially the United States) identified in varying degrees with Israel.

Two dangers seem paramount in the current Middle East crisis. First, resumption of war between Israel and Egypt could lead to further Soviet intervention, eventually compelling an American response and the danger of confrontation. Second, the unsettled Arab world will probably continue its drift towards policies more favorable to the Soviet Union if only by virtue of their extreme antagonism to the West. Thus, the dangers of disaster are compounded by an increasingly radical trend in the Arab world.

Opportune deployment of increased Soviet conventional power in the Middle East—in the changing global strategic context—has brought the Soviet Union considerable advantage. Whether this advantage is to be pressed will be indicated by Soviet tactics along the Suez Canal, for if the Soviets are determined to risk confrontation, then President Nixon's fear that the Middle East is the region where the danger of war is paramount will be justified.

Soviet support [22] of the newly formed federation of Arab republics (comprised of the UAR, Syria and Libya) is almost certain to lessen chances for a peace settlement, since Egypt and Israel are less likely to reach a separate agreement as long as the Egyptian negotiating position is linked to more extreme governments. In the event of renewed Egyptian-Israeli hostilities, would the Soviet

---

[21] In addition to the well-publicized SAM anti-aircraft capabilities, the Soviet Union has supplied Egypt with heavy artillery. Since the beginning of 1971, it has also deployed more advanced fighters and airborne fire control systems. In fact, the air defense of Egypt depends primarily upon Soviet-supplied and Soviet-manned equipment.

[22] "The Soviet Union hailed the Arab move as a major gain toward victory over 'aggression, Zionism and neocolonialism,' and the Arab world saw in the federation new strength against Israel." (*New York Times,* April 19, 1971, p. 1.)

Union tolerate another Arab defeat, with its own personnel directly involved? If the answer to this question were negative, it could lead, because of direct Soviet participation, to a U.S.-Soviet confrontation unless Israel agrees to the Soviet-Arab diplomatic position of total withdrawal. Whether this conflict escalates will depend upon the evaluations made in both Washington and Moscow concerning the political implications of the Soviet strategic posture.

Other implications of the lengthening shadow of Soviet military power in both Europe and the Middle East as well as in other regions of the globe, particularly Latin America, are discussed in Appendix B.

Global Issues

Arms Control

Over the past decade, the United States and the Soviet Union have accepted several limited measures of arms control, including an agreement on nuclear weapons in orbit, the Test Ban Treaty, the Non-Proliferation Treaty and, in February 1971, a treaty prohibiting the placing of strategic nuclear weapons on the seabed. In addition, since the autumn of 1969, the two superpowers have been engaged in the Strategic Arms Limitation Talks (SALT). The main issues in these talks are (1) the definition of strategic arms, (2) types of limitations on such weapons, and (3) methods of verification.

The USSR's motives in arms control are numerous. Its reasons for favoring an agreement may include a desire to escape from the "economics of futility" in the arms race; to "freeze" the existing relationship of nuclear forces between the powers; to prevent proliferation; to symbolize U.S.-Soviet "condominium"; to slow the U.S. deployment of advanced weapons systems while the Soviet Union registers technological advances; and to reduce the confidence of European allies in the U.S. guarantee by establishing negotiating frameworks excluding European interests. Any analysis of Soviet arms control policy, however, reveals Soviet sensitivity to the political uses of military power.

Soviet insistence upon defining U.S. fighter bombers in Europe (the NATO deterrent) as strategic while excluding Soviet I-MRBMs targeted against Western Europe, for instance, would degrade the NATO deterrent without reducing the vulnerability of Western Europe. In addition, Soviet negotiating proposals, centering thus far on the limitation of ABMs to Washington and Moscow, appear designed to "perpetuate" the present strategic balance whereby the Soviet Union has a considerable counterforce capability while we have largely a countercity strategic force. Since the resulting balance, if these proposals were accepted, would eliminate the U.S. residual strategic force save as a last effort counterretaliation, the Soviet strategic posture translates into local Soviet superiority in the "operating dimensions" of international politics—below the nuclear threshold.

For the USSR, an agreed arms control formula which halts further quantitative deployment in offensive systems is more desirable than one which prevents qualitative improvement of existing weapons. For example, the Soviet Union now leads significantly in land-based missiles.[23]

---

[23] Even assuming that the agreement would permit future qualitative upgrading of strategic weapons, the Soviet Union might not unreasonably expect that the U.S. government will encounter greater political difficulty in the effort to sustain qualitative improvements during the years ahead.

At the same time, the Soviet Union seeks to prevent the deployment of the American ABM because the Safeguard system would reduce the quantitative advantage of the Soviet counterforce (SS-9) capability. It is in the realm of ABM technology, along with that of MIRV and penetration aids, that the United States still maintains a precarious and diminishing lead, and where any deployment delay aids the Soviet Union's strategic advance. The motives, definition and type of limitation converge in the issue of verification. For instance, a limitation on MIRVs cannot be supervised by means short of ground inspection, but new missile silos *under construction* can be observed by satellite.[24] At this point, both sides want arms control subject to independent national inspection, thereby avoiding either the controversy of international "inspectors" or visits of foreign nationals to secret establishments. Such a position, however, lends itself more to verification of a *quantitative agreement than a qualitative* arrangement which prohibits technical advances. The ability of the United States to enter a strategic arms agreement compatible with national security depends largely upon an estimate of U.S. ability to restore a balanced relationship between U.S. and Soviet strategic capabilities through qualitative improvements. Simultaneously, the United States and its allies must be able to match Soviet conventional forces in the post-SALT era.

If the Soviet leadership is pursuing the opportunity strategy, then the SALT lose much of their urgency. If American strategic arms programs are delayed in anticipation of a "successful" outcome of the talks, the acceleration of the Soviet programs increases the Soviet Union's favorable position. In this formula, the basic Soviet proposals suggest either restrictions on the deployment of weaponry where the United States has advantages (such as ABM) or numerical freezes whose operating definition damages NATO (inclusion of European-based fighter bombers). A Soviet effort, as suggested in Brezhnev's speech to the 24th party congress, to convene, under UN auspices, a conference on nuclear armaments reduction by the five nuclear powers would vastly complicate the problem of East-West agreement. Under such circumstances, the SALT would become either the instrument of tactical delay or the forum for ratification of Soviet military advantages.

Should Soviet policymakers be more "cautious," they would avoid bringing the talks to a deadlock. Although this tactic could be countenanced even in an opportunity strategy, the "cautious" assumption involves an estimate by the Soviet Union that time is not necessarily on its side. Some agreement, therefore, would be desirable, especially if it preserved a strategic relationship favorable to Soviet operations below the nuclear threshold. The assessment implies that it is too soon for Soviet leaders to decide how favorable that relationship is. Consequently, it is too risky for them to presume that lengthy but inconclusive negotiations are not damaging to their own security.

Finally, a condominium strategy would seek to establish a SALT agreement that recognized Soviet equality in international politics. A strategic arms agree-

---

[24] It is important to note that a completed and camouflaged silo cannot be discovered by satellite observation.

ment appropriate to this circumstance would pledge to preserve basic "parity" between the powers at the nuclear level. The more important function of the agreement, however, could be an implicit link with international politics below the strategic level where the Soviet Union would be free to assert its "equality" in all regions. Hence, the Soviet Union would have an interest in as permanent a quantitative or qualitative freeze as it could obtain. It is not clear, however, that the Soviet government has concluded that an agreement would be more beneficial than further strategic expansion, a consideration which may account for the cautious and exploratory nature of Soviet proposals.

Whether from the Soviet perspective the SALT are merely a temporary tactic or the potential foundation agreement heralding a new era, these talks symbolize the attainment by the Soviet Union of a status as a nuclear power equal to that of the United States. From this recognition, combined with the impression of pending U.S. withdrawal (Europe and Asia) or Soviet ascendancy (Middle East), comes an enormous gain of prestige.

From such a prestigious position, the Soviet Union can approach SALT by combining or modifying the three postulated strategies. The requirements for maximizing Soviet interests will vary from time to time and therefore it is impractical to predetermine which model the Soviet policymakers are going to follow in a particular case. This is especially true since Kremlin decisionmakers are not accountable to public opinion and therefore have more options and greater maneuverability than U.S. policymakers.

United Nations and International Organization

At no time since its founding has the future contribution of the United Nations to international security been more uncertain than at the beginning of the 1970s. The great power dispute over the financing of the Congo operation in the early 1960s and the withdrawal of the UN Emergency Force from Egypt on the eve of the Six-Day War in June 1967 have undermined the UN's utility as a peacekeeping agency. The lesson of these experiences is that the United Nations cannot be effective in the face of great power disagreement. With few exceptions, the great powers prefer to negotiate among themselves rather than to employ the agency of the Secretariat or the forum of the General Assembly.

Whatever their differences with respect to the UN's role in peacekeeping, the United States and the Soviet Union are apparently cooperating in two areas created by technological developments of the last twenty years. Outer space and the seabed are potent sources of wealth and strategic advantage. In both, the United Nations has attempted to foster a claim on behalf of the "international community."

The United States and the Soviet Union, eventually joined by over 100 states, have agreed in the Outer Space Treaty (1967) to refrain from orbiting or stationing in space any weapons of mass destruction and from establishing military bases, testing weapons or conducting military maneuvers on celestial bodies. In

19

addition, they have agreed that outer space is to be free for exploration and use by all states. Nonetheless, the Soviet Union is developing a satellite capable of destroying other outer space vehicles [25] and its fractional orbital bombardment system infringes upon the spirit if not on the letter of the agreement.

On February 11, 1971, the United States and the Soviet Union joined 61 other nations in signing a treaty banning the placement of weapons of mass destruction on the ocean floor beyond a 12-mile coastal zone. Under the provisions of the pact, each signatory has a right to verify the activities of the other parties on the seabed. The current technological ability of the Soviet Union to exploit the seabed for military purposes is undoubtedly less than current American capabilities in this area. Thus Soviet leaders relinquished very little in return for the denial of the use of the seabed to the United States. Moreover, the treaty affords them the opportunity to champion the rights of the "international community" over those who have the greatest ability to exploit the seabed's resources. Whether or not the Soviet Union was motivated to sign this treaty by a strategy of "opportunity," "caution," or "condominium" will be difficult to ascertain until it acquires and exercises a greater oceanic technological capability.

Open and Closed Societies

It has been an article of faith in the West that the "open" society can survive any lengthy contest with a closed society. This conviction derives from an estimate that closed societies lack convenient or viable channels for change or correction of social ills. Hence, although the open society may appear less cohesive than its adversary, its inner allegiance is stronger for being given freely than the imposed cohesion of the closed society's dictatorship or oligarchy. How are these propositions faring?

The Soviet Union, while it possesses military power as never before, also faces major problems complicating the successful conduct of foreign policy. As an ideology, communism purports to be internationalist. Nevertheless, the Soviet government rules a vast multinational state which is beset by formidable nationality problems. The appeal of communism, far from being universal, is so limited that the Soviet Union had to intervene in Hungary (1956) and Czechoslovakia (1968) with vast military power and adopt the Brezhnev Doctrine designed to legitimize such intervention in the future on behalf of "socialist" internationalism. The East European regimes, and more specifically the Czechoslovak "counter-revolution," represent a continuing source of weakness and apprehension to the Soviet Union. The East European problem is repeated within the Soviet Union itself, where the Great Russians rule in the name of the Communist Party and where members of Soviet minorities, including the Jews, also find themselves oppressed. In addition, the plight of Russian Jewry is aggravated by Soviet Middle East policy and historical anti-Semitism.

Although practical men are the chief governors and administrators of this

---

[25] The *Guardian* (Manchester), November 3, 1970, p. 1; see also *The Times* (London), December 2, 1970.

world, men of ideas often shape their actions. In the communist world, ideological fervor seems to be eroding and Marxist-Leninist doctrine appears to have decreasing intellectual appeal. General intellectual dissatisfaction with the philosophical underpinnings of the Soviet regime, even if it does not extend to the socialist system of production, must be a serious concern of the Soviet ruling elite since it could weaken popular allegiance to that regime.

Deficiencies in economic performance furnish another series of difficult problems for the Soviet leadership. The purchase of entire consumer goods plants abroad, a general lack of growth capital and inefficient technology for consumer goods industries remain the price of rapid advances in military technology. The speeches of Soviet officials reveal the Soviet government's awareness of "rising expectations" on the part of the population but provide no evidence that the means to respond effectively to such demands has been discovered.[26]

The current leadership of the Soviet Union holds none of the charismatic, romantic qualities so attractive to the foreign revolutionaries whose support Moscow desires. Nonetheless, there can be very little question of the patriotism (at least among the Great Russians, who represent about half the Soviet Union's population) which sustains the Soviet government. The prospects of improved economic conditions and heightened political and scientific prestige serve to unite most of the Soviet people. The Soviet system can be justified so long as the Soviet government can explain domestic deficiencies by reference to foreign threats and can hold forth reasonable expectation of economic and political success. Soviet scientific dissidents do not appear sufficiently numerous or popular to be able to challenge the very structure and existence of the system. Nor is it clear that they seek fundamental social change. On the other hand, the Soviet literary intelligentsia is indeed strongly disaffected and this is likely to generate the greatest Soviet internal problem of the next decade or two.

In contrast, Western societies, the "open" ones, seem increasingly to be beset with basic questions of mass allegiance. Their artists and intellectuals have become alienated from the political systems which have nurtured and sustained their creative efforts. The resulting "separation of wills" has two devastating effects. First, very difficult problems such as race relations are further exacerbated by the paralysis of divided people and divided government. Second, a critical check is placed upon the conduct of consistent foreign policy, both in *appearance* to the foreigner and in *reality* to the statesman. When other states can count upon public divisions in their dealings with the United States, they can, in effect, appeal over an administration's head in foreign policy. In the United States this problem is complicated by the constitutional separation of powers among the branches of government, most notably between the President and the Congress. Dangerous conclusions may be drawn from the fact of public disorder and the appearance that the United States lacks the capacity and will to resist both domestic and

---

26 The Soviet Union has never been consumer oriented; but it would appear that the Soviet system would have to produce some gradual improvement in order to sustain party control over the citizenry (the stick-and-carrot approach).

foreign challenges. Such a perception—or misperception—can have a highly destabilizing effect on international politics. It was a faulty German estimate of British will which contributed decisively to both World War I and II, and a communist miscalculation of American will which precipitated the Korean conflict and the Cuban missile crisis.

Advancing Technology and Economic Influence

The significance of modern technology for international relations lies in its supreme position as the lever for economic advance and military improvement. Although the Soviet Union has achieved excellence in its military effort, its civilian technology remains backward and defective. Whether the reasons are related to poor organization or lack of incentives, Soviet technological capability remains grossly uneven. The scientific and technological means of the communist world are greatly inferior to those of the United States and its allies. Yet the inability of the latter to concert their efforts more effectively enhances the technological strength of the Soviet Union. Because of the priority which the Soviet Union accords military technology in national planning programs, automobile plants and other such installations for producing consumer goods were purchased from states—such as Italy, West Germany and Japan—which lie within the U.S. security system. The technology which makes possible the Soviet strategic-military program is purchased at great cost to the rest of the economy. The sheer limitation of available resources gives Soviet policymakers one strong motive both for arms control and the condominium policy.

The Soviet press and leadership have frequently boasted that the superiority of their system will be manifested in successful economic competition. Meanwhile, the Soviet government's first priority seems to be superiority in the most advanced military and space technologies. To some extent, the industrialized Western nations, despite their superior consumer economies, are under pressure to avoid or ignore Soviet achievements in the military realm. This pressure is especially telling when it leads to further disruption in the poorly coordinated trade, strategic and economic policies of the countries of the West. The possibility of successful recourse by the United States to "superior technology" as a shortcut or "fix" for diplomatic or military error is fast disappearing. In fact, the declining U.S. effort in R&D increases the prospects for the kind of technological surprise that is exemplified in the Soviet launching of the first sputnik in 1957. Failure to maintain its competitive position on the frontiers of scientific research and technological development reduces the ability of the United States to respond effectively to Soviet advances. A disorganized and declining R&D program cannot be revived immediately, even by the most prodigious efforts, because of the lead time between scientific discovery, technological application and industrial production.

Conclusions

We are not bent on conquest or on threatening others. But we do have a nuclear umbrella that can protect others, above all the states to which we are allied or in which we have great national interest. This is the moral force behind our position. We could become a terrible threat to the world if we were to lose that restraint or if we were to sacrifice our own power and allow ourselves to become too weak to uphold the weak.

Richard M. Nixon
March 9, 1971

In this study, we have attempted to assess the potential implications of Soviet military capabilities and to relate current Soviet policy emphases to the growth of those capabilities. We have found that the nuclear protection provided by U.S. strategic forces to our friends and allies is being reduced by the vast increase in Soviet military capabilities. In addition, the Soviet Union appears to be developing naval and air forces capable of projecting its political influence on a global scale.

Through its superior conventional strength and growing nuclear forces, the Soviet Union is enjoying the status quo in Eastern Europe, while maneuvering to keep Western Europe divided and to strengthen forces friendly to the Soviet Union. Soviet influence and presence are expanding in the Mediterranean, in the Middle East and in the Indian Ocean. Through skillful manipulation of local conflict and direct military intervention along the Suez Canal, the Soviet Union is bidding for control of the old British imperial route to the Indian Ocean and Far East. Whether the purpose of this policy is to obtain leverage against European and Japanese oil sources in the Persian Gulf, to assemble the forces and alliances necessary to contain Communist China, or simply to replace declining American or Western influence remains to be seen. Meanwhile, the Soviets are doing nothing to lesson tensions in the Middle East or Southeast Asia. Instead, they are extending their political and military influence by seeking naval and air bases in those regions.

This policy is paralleled in Latin America where an embryonic Soviet Caribbean fleet is based at Cienfuegos, Cuba. The political trends in the Southern hemisphere—anti-American and revolutionary—favor Soviet activities which have the effect, at the least, of restricting future U.S. flexibility in dealing with crises like Cuba (1962) and the Dominican Republic (1965). Recent Soviet nuclear submarine visits to Cuba have violated the spirit if not the letter of the 1962

23

agreement between President Kennedy and Premier Khrushchev not to station Soviet offensive missiles in Cuba.[27]

What policy emphasis will the Soviet Union adopt? The Soviet leadership could take advantage of the military weakness and public divisions in the West by adopting an opportunity strategy. Alternatively, it may find itself compelled to decide between pressing an opportunity strategy against the West or seeking condominium with the West, in order to prepare against a threat from China. Finally, it may conclude that the caution strategy is least likely to frighten the West and will, at the same time, provide maximum advantage for Soviet political gains—whether these are at the expense of the United States or in preparation against the Chinese, or both.

It is most likely that the Soviet Union will continue its past performance of alternating and combining these approaches, as the situation warrants. This task is made easier by the existence of many more military options than it has ever possessed. The uncertainty associated with nuclear deterrence cannot check a calculated, incremental extension of Soviet foreign policy interests and commitments, buttressed by conventional military presence and an ever more powerful strategic nuclear force. Even the most cautious and least pretentious of the tendencies in Soviet foreign policy presumes the growth of Soviet power and influence in areas from which the Soviet Union has been historically excluded— from the Middle East to Southeast Asia to Latin America. The Soviet Union stands ready, as never before, to complement and consolidate the political gains of the indirect approach by military might.

Those who wish the United States to avoid this prospect in the face of growing Soviet strategic power are concerned especially about the decline in national morale caused by the Indochina war. Both Presidents Truman (in 1953) and Johnson (in 1969) retired from political life because they took measures, respectively, in North and Southeast Asia to resist what they considered to be communist aggression. In neither of these cases, however, were Soviet military forces employed, although Soviet military and financial support was crucial to both.[28] These precedents dramatically illustrate the limitations inherent in the polarization of the American people on questions of foreign affairs: the ultimate limitation is the threat to a President's continuation in office if his concept of the national interest compels him to commit large numbers of American troops in areas where Soviet forces are not directly involved. Thus, the failure of the United States to counter the "indirect" application of Soviet military resources is complicated by the problem of a growing Soviet military presence deriving from the USSR's increased capabilities.

A leading Soviet student of American affairs, G. A. Arbatov (director, Institute for the Study of the USA, Moscow), analyzed the contemporary U.S. mood in a recent article on American foreign policy prospects for the 1970s:

---

[27] See Appendix B for fuller analyses of these developments.
[28] Hundreds of thousands of Chinese peoples' volunteers, however, fought in the Korean War against the U.S. and UN forces.

A situation has arisen in which continuation or, beyond that, further activation of a policy aimed at strengthening the military might and international influence of the United States is beginning, in the opinion of many sober Americans, to threaten serious domestic complications and the undermining of the foundations of the "national power of the USA." From this derive the deep differences in the ruling circles themselves, in the "political elite" as such.[29]

The reluctance of many Americans to cope with the world beyond U.S. borders could be read by Soviet policymakers as presenting opportunities to alter the global balance of power, to fragment our alliances, and to threaten U.S. security itself.

Growing American incapacity and irresolution before Soviet advances is already making the United States a questionable partner for those who must risk our friendship as an alternative to accommodation with the Soviet Union. The United States can have no policy save retreat if it is unable or unwilling to maintain political commitments with a defense capability sufficient to deter the Soviet Union from *political* exploitation of the vast Soviet military establishment.

Yet in recent years, we have sought to achieve security at "bargain rates." The proof of this can be seen in the continuous decline in the portion of our ever-expanding GNP that is committed to national defense—in contrast to the steady increase in comparable Soviet expenditures. Although the wide margin of superiority we enjoyed over the Soviet Union a decade ago has, until recently, sustained the psychological appearance of U.S. advantage, we have failed to recognize that national security and international peace cannot be bought cheaply. The United States may have forgotten the maxim that there is room for only one at the top. Leonid Brezhnev's declaration to the 24th party congress—"the total triumph of socialism the world over is inevitable"—reminds us that the Soviet Union wants to be that one.

---

[29] *SShA: ekonomika, politika, ideologiia,* 1970, No. 1, p. 19 (translated and printed in *Soviet Law and Government,* Summer 1970, pp. 3-27).

Appendix A

Comparative U.S. and Soviet Military Forces

The rapid growth of Soviet strategic power during the last decade is depicted in Figures 1 and 2. The material therein does not reflect the total advantage of the Soviet Union in missile strength relative to the United States since it does not encompass the megatonnage aspect of such strength.

The Soviet Union has already deployed a limited anti-ballistic missile defense. Its construction of SLBMs is proceeding at a rapid enough rate so that its SLBM forces will equal U.S. Polaris forces by 1974. The Soviet space program, which emphasizes unmanned remote control activity, has already tested weapons systems designed to destroy and defend reconnaissance satellites. At a time of uncertainty about the future of the post-Apollo program, the Soviet Union appears to be allocating resources for a technological capability to probe far into outer-space. In conventional weapons systems, the Soviet Union has made impressive advances in both radar and missile system air defenses.

Currently, the U.S. military establishment is in a period of constriction. The United States has produced strategic innovations, including MIRVs (especially on the Polaris-Poseidon), and is slowly deploying a potentially more effective ABM system. The trend of U.S. defense expenditures, however, is to continue at current levels, with a considerable reduction of conventional forces in the wake of withdrawal from Vietnam.

Conventionally, the Soviet Navy will continue to grow in quality and size (see Figure 3). The Soviet Union has the largest submarine force in the world. The attack submarine force of the USSR and its Warsaw Pact allies exceeds that of NATO, 112 to 80, respectively.[1] The Soviet Navy does lack sufficient sea and land-based air support.

By 1974 the Soviet Union can be expected to possess interceptors and strike fighters equal or superior to our own. The pace of Soviet activity in the design and production of fighter aircraft far exceeds our own. New Soviet fighters have been introduced about every 18 months. The U.S. will not have a new fighter aircraft until about 1975, and this fighter, according to the Defense Department's Director of Research and Engineering, may provide a margin of superiority.[2]

---

[1] For further details, see *The Military Balance 1970-1971* (London: The Institute for Strategic Studies, 1970), p. 96.
[2] Statement by Dr. John Foster, September 1970.

27

Figure 4 indicates the Warsaw Pact's conventional advantage over NATO forces. The main comparisons are in troop strength, armor, artillery and tactical aircraft. Although the troop formations are not comparable because of numerous differences among them, the figures as presented indicate NATO's general conventional inferiority. In addition to outnumbering NATO considerably in the vital Northern and Central European fronts, the Warsaw Pact enjoys nearly a three-to-one advantage in main battle tanks and a five-to-three advantage in tactical aircraft. NATO relies upon higher quality aircraft capable of both conventional and tactical nuclear roles. However, new Soviet fighter designs may jeopardize this qualitative advantage. Finally, the Warsaw Pact uses mostly standardized Soviet equipment, while NATO logistics are still supplied by many national sources.

Figure 5 demonstrates the rapid growth of Soviet R&D compared to the stationary or declining U.S. effort. The significance of R&D is that it presages the future. What appears as a small lag, year by year, eventuates in a great cumulative difference. Advanced technology is the growth capital of military power.

It should be noted that the R&D described here is state-supported. On the other hand, the R&D gap for civilian goods between the United States and the Soviet Union continues to increase to the advantage of the United States.

Figure 1

TRENDS IN U.S. AND SOVIET
OPERATIONAL ICBM LAUNCHERS

Number of Launchers

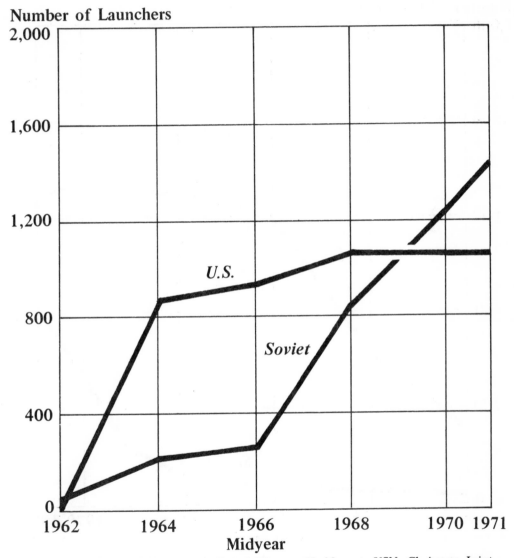

Midyear

Source: Statement by Admiral Thomas H. Moorer, USN, Chairman Joint Chiefs of Staff, before the House Armed Services Committee, March 9, 1971.

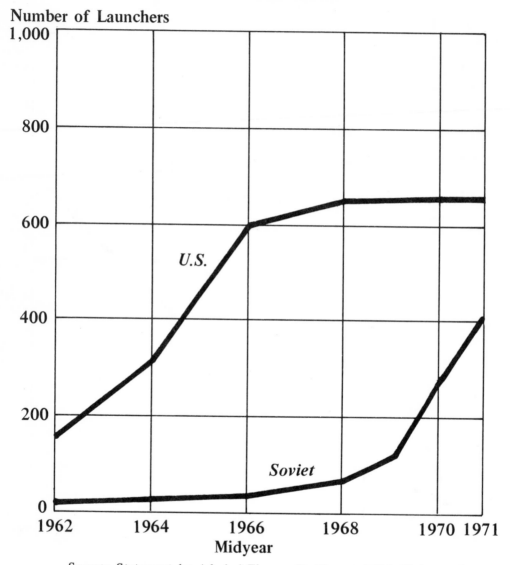

Figure 2

**TRENDS IN U.S. AND SOVIET
OPERATIONAL SLBM LAUNCHERS**

Number of Launchers

Source: Statement by Admiral Thomas H. Moorer, USN, Chairman Joint
Chiefs of Staff, before the House Armed Services Committee, March 9, 1971.

Figure 3

UNITED STATES AND SOVIET FLEETS

(Approximate figures from unclassified data)

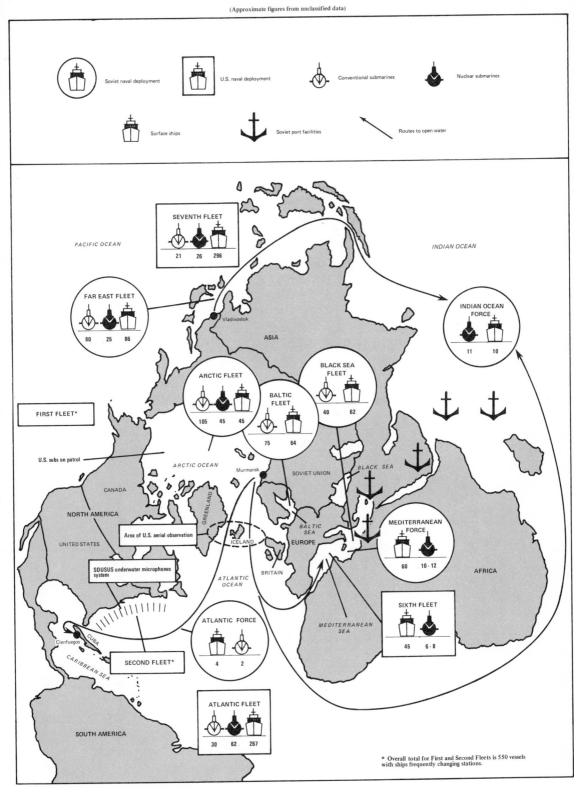

Source: *New York Times,* Sunday, March 14, 1971, Section 4, p.3.

31

Figure 4

NATO-WARSAW PACT CONVENTIONAL STRENGTH

Category	Northern and Central Europe			Southern Europe		
	NATO	Warsaw Pact	(of which USSR)	NATO	Warsaw Pact	(of which USSR)
Combat and direct support troops available (000s)	580[1]	900	585	525	370	75
Main battle tanks available to commanders—in peacetime	5,500	14,000	8,000	2,100	5,000	1,400
Tactical aircraft in operational service:						
—light bombers	16	240	200	—	30	30
—fighter/ground attack	1,400	1,300	1,000	600	200	50
—interceptors	350	2,000	900	250	850	450
—reconnaissance	400	400	300	100	100	40

[1] If French forces are included the NATO figure for Northern and Central Europe would be increased by perhaps 40,000.
Source: Adapted from *The Military Balance 1970-1971* (London: The Institute for Strategic Studies, 1970), pp. 90-95.

Figure 5

U.S.-SOVIET RESEARCH, DEVELOPMENT, TEST, ENGINEERING AND SPACE EXPENDITURES
(current prices)

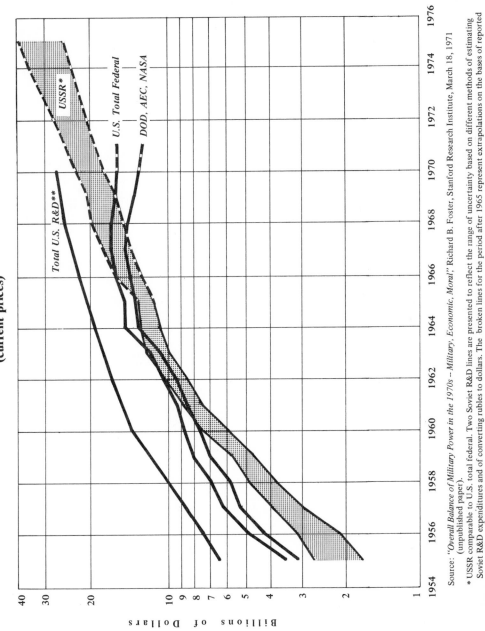

Source: *"Overall Balance of Military Power in the 1970s – Military, Economic, Moral,"* Richard B. Foster, Stanford Research Institute, March 18, 1971 (unpublished paper).

* USSR comparable to U.S. total federal. Two Soviet R&D lines are presented to reflect the range of uncertainty based on different methods of estimating Soviet R&D expenditures and of converting rubles to dollars. The broken lines for the period after 1965 represent extrapolations on the bases of reported Soviet allocations. These lines are likely to underestimate actual Soviet R&D expenditures.

** Total U.S. R&D excludes most investment in R&D facilities.

Appendix B
Regional Implications

In the following sections, the major political trends in each region of the world are discussed and the implications of growing Soviet military power are assessed. Contrasting U.S. and Soviet interests, strategies, and goals are set forth. In addition, each region is evaluated in the light of alternative Soviet strategies set forth in the second chapter of this study.

Europe

The principal issues in contemporary European politics derive from the division of the European continent after the Second World War. They are: (1) the German question and the status of Berlin; (2) political trends in NATO-Europe, including both West European integration and the existence of political difficulties in such countries as Turkey, Greece and Italy which may create formidable problems for NATO's southern flank; (3) political and economic problems in Eastern Europe, especially in those which pose a threat to communist political systems, e.g., Poland and Czechoslovakia; and (4) the threat to NATO's southern flank and Europe's energy sources posed by the loss of Western influence in the Middle East.

The most immediate effect of the increased military strength of the Soviet Union has been to reduce the efficacy of NATO's "flexible response" strategy. This strategy envisages a Warsaw Pact incursion being met, initially at least, by NATO conventional forces. Only if such a response should fail to halt a Warsaw Pact invasion would nuclear weapons be used. Since NATO's conventional forces have been inferior to the opposing Eastern armies, especially since the Soviet invasion of Czechoslovakia in 1968, the possibility of an early nuclear response to conventional attack has been discussed. But this option is unattractive because: (1) the Soviet Union's medium-range (I-MRBM) missiles and advanced air defense systems offset the fighter-bomber forces which constitute Western Europe's main deterrent; (2) the U.S. strategic (ICBM and SLBM) deterrent which protects both the United States and Western Europe has been weakened as Soviet strategic forces have grown; and (3) NATO's tactical nuclear weapons, should they be used against a Soviet conventional attack, would devastate large populated areas of Germany. The European states have progressed little in providing both conventional forces and modern weapon systems, such as battlefield sensors and air superiority fighters, to improve their conventional forces. Thus, at a time when the Soviet Union possesses calculable strategic advantage against Western Europe,

35

both the effectiveness of NATO strategy and its "linkage" to U.S. nuclear power are in question.

The withdrawal of U.S. conventional forces, which certain members of the U.S. Senate have urged, would diminish still further the expectation that the United States would use strategic capabilities in defense of Western Europe. As U.S. forces were withdrawn, the tangible evidence of the U.S. commitment to Europe would be reduced; consequently, the U.S. nuclear guarantee to Europe would become less credible. Thus, in this period of U.S.-Soviet strategic parity, pressures for the unilateral reduction of U.S. troops in Europe could scarcely arise at a less advantageous time from the U.S. perspective.

Undoubtedly, changes in the U.S.-Soviet strategic relationship, together with pressures for the reduction of U.S. conventional forces, have contributed to a rising West European interest in a political settlement with the Soviet Union. *Ostpolitik,* pursued by the German government, represents an effort to improve relations between the Federal Republic, the Soviet Union and Eastern Europe. Specifically, *Ostpolitik* has consisted of a series of bilateral efforts between West Germany and the Soviet Union as well as between Bonn and various East Central European communist states: West Germany has tentatively "acknowledged" the Oder-Niesse line; Chancellor Brandt has negotiated with the East German government without recognizing it diplomatically; and the Soviet government has indicated a keen interest in acquiring access to West German advanced technology to assist in the modernization of the Soviet economy. In predicating the ratification of the German-Soviet treaty of August 1970 on the resolution of East-West differences over the status of Berlin, the Brandt government can be viewed as seeking further assurances of Soviet good behavior. At the same time the Soviet Union has lost no opportunities in its quest either for political position or for technologically advantageous economic arrangements.

From the Soviet perspective, the *Ostpolitik*, the Moscow-Bonn treaty of August 1970, and the idea of a conference on European security may be seen as ploys to obtain international recognition of a permanent Soviet sphere of influence, while continuing to labor for the detachment of West Germany from NATO and the European Community. The Soviet government is in an excellent position to wait out American troop withdrawals without making concessions to Western Europe. At the same time, the Brezhnev Doctrine provides the Soviet Union with ideological justification for recourse to force should Bonn's *Ostpolitik* pose a threat to Soviet control in Eastern Europe as may have occurred prior to August 1968 in Czechoslovakia.

The decline in the effectiveness of NATO and the erosion of the U.S. strategic position have been cause for grave concern in West Germany. Because of a geographic position and economic power potential that make it a prime objective for the Soviet Union, the German Federal Republic is likely to seek an accommodation with the Soviet Union while sufficient U.S. presence remains in Europe to underwrite Bonn's bargaining position. These German sentiments are being cautiously exploited by the Soviet government. Time, however, is an important factor that Soviet policymakers must reckon with. In order to maximize the Soviet advantage, they must reach an accommodation with Bonn before European integration becomes irreversible. Reduced German support and participation in West European political institutions can be regarded as an essential precondition for affirmative Soviet responses to the *Ostpolitik,* since the Soviet Union will hardly benefit from the creation of a politically and economically united rival in Western Europe.

On NATO's southern perimeter, potential political changes in Italy and Turkey could pose major problems for NATO. Continued political instability in Italy could lead to the formation of a coalition government that included the Italian Communist Party, already in control of many local governmental units. Internal political cleavages in Turkey, together with the rapprochement between Turkey and the Soviet Union since the Cyprus crisis of the early 1960s, have already weakened NATO's southeastern flank. While President Tito remains firmly in power at the age of 79, his passing will leave a political void, which may not be filled by the "collective presidency" now being formed. The disintegrative tendencies in Yugoslavia represented by Serbian and Croatian nationalism and the political instability which might accompany a Yugoslav succession crisis would provide opportunities for the Soviet Union in Southeastern Europe. In the Mediterranean the Soviet Fleet, although still inferior to the U.S. Sixth Fleet, gives the Soviet Union additional leverage on future developments in Italy, Greece, Turkey and Yugoslavia. The strategic significance of these countries is apparent. The strengthening of Soviet control over Yugoslavia would undermine "liberalizing" tendencies in other East European states. The assumption of power in Italy by a coalition government with communist participation would weaken NATO's southern flank. Such a government could gravely impair the operation of the European Economic Community, since Italy would probably withdraw from active participation in European integration efforts. The U.S. naval position in the Mediterranean would be weakened with adverse consequences for Greece and Turkey and for the U.S. position in the Middle East.

In this situation, Soviet options are as follows:

(1) If the Soviet Union chooses to pursue a policy of *opportunity,* it will not be unduly concerned that coercive tactics in Eastern Europe will make its relations with Western Europe more difficult; the West Europeans will have no choice but to negotiate from weakness, given the strategic decline of NATO. Nor would the Soviet Union hesitate to intervene (not necessarily with military force) in Southern Europe as a party vitally interested in the Yugoslav succession and the political future of Italy.

The aim of such a policy would be the diminution of U.S. influence and ultimately the expulsion of the United States from Europe and the thwarting of European political unity.

(2) By adopting a policy of *caution,* the Soviet Union could pursue a similar end, with the essential difference that it would take greater care to avoid a provocation of NATO or the United States. The policy of caution relies less upon the military option as the "shadow" over negotiations. The cautious attitude, however, allows Eastern Europe to remain an area of Soviet hegemony.

(3) A policy of *condominium* once again need not diminish Soviet control over Eastern Europe. But the Soviet aim in Western Europe would be less to diminish or expel U.S. influence than to "stabilize" U.S. support behind a Europe which is neither a political nor military competitor of the Soviet Union. Hence, a Conference on European Security, *Ostpolitik* and the arms control talks would be designed to maintain a status quo, perhaps emerging ultimately in a European security treaty backed by a joint U.S.-Soviet guarantee. This political and military status quo would then serve Soviet interests, especially since the Soviet Union would have secured a position of strength on NATO's southern flank.

The Middle East and Persian Gulf

Strategically situated as a bridgehead linking Europe, Asia and Africa, the Middle East has long been a traditional object of Russian diplomacy. In recent times, the region's great oil reserves have become crucial to Western Europe and Japan. Its impoverished population, its political rivalries and religious disputes, complicated above all by the Arab-Israeli conflict, present fertile opportunities for maneuver. Moreover, the existence of Israel, with its attraction to Russian Jewry, poses difficulties for the Soviet Union in its own domestic minority policies. As the aspiring protector of Pan-Arabist policies emanating from Cairo, the Soviet government reaps advantages which are denied to Western powers and especially to the United States—identified as they are, in varying degrees, with Israel.

Since 1967, the Soviet Union has acted in a dual capacity: as the diplomatic spokesman for the militant Arabs in the Four-Power talks, and the principal military backer of the Egyptians in the "war of attrition." In 1970 the "war of attrition" went badly when the Egyptians, having begun the war with artillery barrages, could not halt the retaliatory raids of the Israeli Air Force. As a consequence, the Soviet Union undertook the creation of an air defense for Egypt and provided Soviet-manned SAMs, MIG fighters, and pilots. Since mid-March 1971, the Soviet Union has shipped its most modern aircraft to Egypt. The Soviet Air Force and Navy have also acquired airfield facilities and ports of call in North Africa and the Middle East as a result of their strong support for the Arab cause.

Two dangers were outlined above as being crucial in the current Middle East crisis. First, the resumption of war between Israel and Egypt could lead to further Soviet intervention, compelling eventually an American response and the danger of confrontation. Second, the unsettled Arab world could continue to drift toward policies more favorable to the Soviets if only by the extreme antagonism of some Arab countries to the West.

The United States has been ineffective in countering either danger. It is obvious that the direct employment of Soviet military power on Egypt's behalf has improved dramatically both the military and diplomatic prospects of the Arabs. The Israelis, supported by the United States, see their diplomatic position compromised and their military margin declining. And while the U.S.-sponsored cease-fire initiative did touch off the Jordanian civil war (which greatly damaged the cause and campaign of the Palestinian guerrillas), Soviet-Egyptian violations of the cease-fire materially improved their "local balance of forces."

The most immediate aim of these Soviet tactics appeared to be the reopening of the Suez Canal and the withdrawal of Israeli forces from its Eastern bank. A reopened Suez Canal could then become the channel for the extension of Soviet influence throughout the Middle East and into the oil-rich and politically unstable Persian Gulf.

The United States is severely hampered under these circumstances, for the Sixth Fleet, the local force at our disposal, now has a growing Soviet Navy to oppose it. The USSR seems to be capitalizing on an opportunity strategy, where both the local balance of forces along the Suez and the nuclear stalemate enable it to create the fear of confrontation, while avoiding a clearly offensive posture. Soviet support of the recently-formed federation of the UAR, Syria and Libya, combined with shipments to Egypt of the most modern Soviet aircraft, emphasize Moscow's basic policy. This is to present the U.S. and Israel with the prospect of an Israeli defeat by Soviet-Arab forces on the battlefield if Israel does not accept Soviet-Arab diplomatic terms. In the event of fresh Egyptian-Israeli hostilities, will Moscow tolerate another Arab defeat, especially with its own personnel involved? Should the Soviet Union intervene massively in the Middle East in an attempt to defeat the Israelis, will the United States stand up to the dreaded confrontation?

Meanwhile, because of Soviet intervention, the political position of the United States in the Arab world cannot profit from either Israeli capitulation or obstinacy, a partial settlement reopening the Suez Canal, or a peace "settlement," except one mutually satisfactory to the contestants.

Opportune employment of increased Soviet conventional power in the Middle East under conditions of nuclear "parity" has brought the Soviet Union considerable advantage. Whether this advantage is to be pressed will be indicated by Soviet policies along the Suez Canal. The Middle East might become the theater of "Cuba in reverse," as one East European diplomat suggested. Then the Soviet Union might gain control of European and Japanese oil supplies and, more importantly, demonstrate Soviet military superiority in any showdown with the United States. The result could well be cataclysmic, as President Nixon has pointed out.

Indian Ocean, South Asia

Britain's decision in 1967 to withdraw its forces from East of Suez was predicated primarily on economic considerations. Although the Heath government has made minor modifications in the policy established by the Wilson government,

Britain will complete her military withdrawal from the Persian Gulf by the end of 1971. For the past several years, British influence in the Indian Ocean has been waning. There is as yet no clear replacement, although Britain, Australia, New Zealand, Singapore and Malaysia have been discussing a new collective security arrangement.

For a variety of reasons the Soviet Union has sought to establish itself throughout the Indian Ocean region.[1] Among these reasons are the following:

(1) The Indian Ocean is the historical maritime trade gateway from the Atlantic to the Pacific. Currently, the most important commodity moving through this gateway is vast quantities of Middle East and Persian Gulf oil destined for Western Europe and Japan.

(2) Whether or not the Suez Canal is reopened, Soviet capabilities in the area and use of the sea routes of the Indian Ocean can facilitate both Soviet reinforcement of North Vietnam and the implementation of a containment policy aimed at China, while simultaneously easing communications between Soviet Black Sea and Far Eastern ports. Thus, the Soviet Union, by establishing a position of great influence in the Indian Ocean and its littoral, may check Chinese expansion southward in much the same fashion as Britain, as an imperial power, sought in the nineteenth century to forestall Tsarist Russian expansion.

(3) A Soviet naval presence is important to the extension of Soviet influence in Pakistan, India, Ceylon and Indonesia.

Whatever the reasons, the Soviet Union is waging a campaign designed to enhance its strategic position in the Indian Ocean. It has sought to achieve political influence combined with basing rights and a naval presence. Toward these ends, the Soviet Union has assisted in the development of port facilities at Hodeida in Yemen and sought anchorage and loading facilities at Aden and Socotra, both useful for controlling the entrance to the Red Sea. A port agreement has been concluded with Mauritius, extensive rights have been secured at Visakhapatnam on the east coast of India, and naval repair contracts have been negotiated in Singapore. Moreover, the Soviet Union has supported rebellions in the weak sheikhdoms along the Persian Gulf. Against these activities, besides the small and over-aged U.S. Indian Ocean squadron, the United States and Britain are establishing a communications facility at Diego Garcia in the Indian Ocean.

Soviet goals in the Indian Ocean would be more easily achieved if the Suez Canal were reopened. In order to protect Red Sea approaches, the Soviet Union has concentrated not only on the Arabian peninsula side, but has also sought to extend its influence on the African flank by courting the favor of Somalia.

Any evaluation of Communist activities in Africa and the Indian Ocean would be incomplete without reference to the progress being made by the People's

---

[1] By asserting that the Indian Ocean is potentially a dangerous deployment area of U.S. Polaris or Poseidon missile submarines aimed at the Soviet heartland, the Russians justify the establishment of a Soviet naval force in the area.

Republic of China in nearby areas. Tanzania has valuable harbor facilities at Dar-es-Salaam. Although the ports of Zanzibar can serve equally well the interests of maritime merchants or naval vessels with primarily Asian missions, Dar-es-Salaam is a valuable gateway to Africa's interior. Tanzania avowedly pursues a nonaligned course, but Chinese activity and aid have been significant. Several years ago, a Chinese-Tanzanian maritime venture was begun. In November 1969 a formal agreement was signed by Zambia, Tanzania and Communist China for the construction of a 1,200-mile railway from Dar-es-Salaam to the Zambian copperbelt region. In addition, China has been the prime supplier of Tanzania's weapons in the recent past. Chinese intrusion into Northeastern Africa in competition with the Soviet Union is likely to contribute to the radicalization of this region at the expense of Western influence.

Closely tied to Soviet policies in the Indian Ocean are its activities in other parts of the African continent. The Soviet Union has an initial advantage in Africa as a major power with no imperial history in the area. Further, it can exploit the issues of white minority rule in Southwest Africa, the Republic of South Africa and Rhodesia—as well as Portuguese conduct in Angola and Mozambique—as the work of the "racist" West. Nor has the Soviet Union abandoned hope of gaining influence along the West African coast. Soviet military aid to the federal government in Nigeria was important to that government's victory over Biafra in the Nigerian civil war.

The growth of the Soviet naval presence in the Indian Ocean has contributed to Britain's decision to resume military aid to South Africa. As part of its 1955 agreement with South Africa for continued use of the Simonstown naval base, Britain has begun to make available weapons designed to strengthen South Africa's naval capabilities in the strategically important Cape shipping lanes. While recognizing the significance of freedom of movement for naval craft in the surrounding seas, black African leaders have strongly criticized the British action as benefiting racist policies. Thus, one result of expanding Soviet naval power has been to complicate racial antagonisms within the British Commonwealth by forcing Britain to safeguard her Cape shipping routes through cooperation with South Africa, whose importance has increased since the closing of the Suez Canal.

The Soviet Union has complemented its naval presence in the Indian Ocean by seeking influence in all major South Asian states. Pakistan receives Soviet military and economic aid. It is too soon to say, however, whether the secessionist movement and civil war in East Pakistan will work to Soviet benefit, particularly since Peking has developed a de facto alliance with Pakistan.

Ceylon faces a grave internal crisis precipitated by the terrorist activities of a guerrilla force, some of whose members have apparently received extensive training in North Korea, a country which is far more closely aligned with the Soviet Union than with China. However, the Soviet Union has also given military assistance to the government of Ceylon in its struggle against the revolutionary forces. Whatever the Soviet role in supporting the insurgency threat in Ceylon,

41

in his speech to the 24th party congress Leonid Brezhnev referred to the "important social changes" occurring in Ceylon. If the Soviet Union has chosen a strategy designed to achieve a position of dominance in the Indian Ocean, Ceylon occupies a geographic position of key importance.

After Egypt, India receives the highest amount of economic assistance from the Soviet Union. The subcontinent is important to Moscow, and it is also crucial to China. The Russians use every opportunity to deflect credit for American successes, while highlighting their own contribution to the Indian people. Moreover, the Indian press perceives a U.S. threat to Indian independence in the area and tends to minimize any threat from the Soviet Union.

At this point, it is too early to judge the implications of the 1971 Indian elections for Soviet policy in India. The broad margin of Mrs. Indira Gandhi's election victory has now obviated any necessity for coalition with the Indian Communist Party. While this must be viewed as a short-term Soviet loss, it does not amount to a fatal setback. Even without such an advantage, however, the USSR can be expected to continue to stress policies designed to strengthen its position in India because of the strategic significance of the Indian subcontinent in the Indian Ocean area. In addition, India could serve as the principal bastion in a Soviet encirclement of China, if that in fact is a Soviet aim.

Southeast Asia

The war-torn peninsula of Southeast Asia provides the land and sea passageway between the Indian Ocean and the Pacific Basin. Just as Suez and the Cape control the entry points from the west, the Malacca Straits at the southern tip of Southeast Asia control entry into the Indian Ocean from the east. Soviet policy, under conditions of nuclear "parity," has been designed to gain a foothold in both the Middle East and Southeast Asia.

Over two years ago, Leonid Brezhnev proposed a new security arrangement for Asia. While the Soviet government has never clarified this statement, it is plain that no state can talk of "balancing" the nuclear China of Mao or aiding the Indians, Pakistanis, Ceylonese or North Vietnamese without military presence or naval access. It is possible to conceive of Soviet policy in Southeast Asia and the Indian Ocean as being a cautious use of the USSR's newly-found military naval capacity to demonstrate Soviet readiness to replace the withdrawing Western security forces. In this scheme, both ports of call and air facilities from Suez to Singapore will be necessary. Where there is no "burning" issue between the United States and the Soviet Union in these areas, the "cautious" or "condominium" emphasis will serve Moscow's interests until the prestige of growing Soviet power replaces the declining Western presence.

The American experience in Vietnam, the manner of U.S. withdrawal, and the success of "Vietnamization" are of crucial importance to all states in the region and to the credibility of U.S. commitments elsewhere in the world. A U.S. political defeat in Southeast Asia, at a time when the United States faces formidable problems both at home and in other regions of the world, would further undermine the confidence of those nations in the United States. Perhaps because of uncertainty about future American policy in Southeast Asia, a number of Southeast Asian nations are beginning to reexamine their foreign policy. President Ferdinand E. Marcos of the Philippines has begun to stress a foreign policy "dictated only by our national interest" and based in part on an "open mind" toward Moscow. Thailand is also in the process of assessing its relationship with the Soviet Union and has given encouragement to overtures from the Soviet Union.

For more than a generation, the United States has contributed to the security of countries located around China's periphery. American power rests not only upon Japan and the Philippines, but on Korea which is strategically important to the Japanese. Given the persistence of tensions between North and South Korea, the interpretation, however inaccurate, that the United States suffered disaster in Vietnam must redound to Chinese benefit. Furthermore, several of these states—Malaya, Thailand, Burma, the Philippines—have nascent or working communist guerrillas. For them, as for Indonesia, the problem of insurgencies actively supported by foreign powers superior to them in strength is unsolved.

Pacific Basin

Events in the Pacific Basin area give grounds for American optimism. Japan, South Korea and the Republic of China on Taiwan are all booming economically and the South Korean and Taiwan governments possess efficient armed forces. At the same time, the Soviet position in the Pacific does not appear as promising as elsewhere. The proximity of China to the area and the relative remoteness of the Soviet-European heartland favor the former power. Of course, cooperation as well as conflict between the two communist giants can be envisaged. At the same time, while the situation may hold promise for polycentric communist advances, Russian gains at the expense of China seem unlikely except, perhaps, in Indonesia. Even after Sukarno's downfall and the near annihilation of the Indonesian Communist Party, once the largest communist party outside the communist world, Indonesia remains a Soviet target country.

Possessing the most productive economy in the region and the third largest on the globe, Japan still remains within the U.S. security system and her foreign and defense policies are governed by this fact. Any conceivable Asian "balance" within the Nixon Doctrine framework must include the Japanese. Because of the doubts surrounding future U.S. strength in the area, the question as to whether the Japanese will act as "independent" partners or as a fully rearmed great power cannot be answered at this time. As an "independent" power, Japan would be in a pivotal position to bid for support from the Soviet Union and China, as well as from the United States. Whatever specific policies the Japanese decide to follow, Japan will emerge as a major political force in great power relations in Asia.

While Japan increasingly trades with her communist neighbors, there are as yet no indications of a political rapprochement which could cause alarm in the

West. Further, while Japan does not seem willing at this point to assume the role of policeman in the area, its potential might is formidable and its national defense forces will grow substantially during the next decade.

Future Japanese policy is complicated by conditions on the Korean peninsula and the island of Taiwan, both crucial to Japanese defense. Tensions remain high between North and South Korea, both of whom possess formidable defense establishments. Yet the South Korean army is deficient in modern equipment and U.S. forces bolstering South Korea's defense are being reduced. In Taiwan, the Nationalist Army and its leader, Generalissimo Chiang Kai-shek, present the problem of unsettled relationships with mainland China. Here again, as in Korea, the Japanese are unsure of future American security policy. Japan has been expanding its trade contacts and investments throughout the world. In particular, it has replaced Britain as Australia's leading trading partner, and the trade of other Asian Commonwealth countries is likely to turn toward Japan if Britain joins the Common Market. It is difficult to predict the precise shape which Japanese economic policy in Asia will assume. Will Japan seek to use its economic power to obtain political advantage? Will Japan develop economic policies which alienate other Asian countries upon whom it is dependent for trade? Will Japan evolve policies which accord with those of the United States?

Australia has until recently regarded itself as threatened only from the north, by island-hopping invaders in a scenario similar to that of the Second World War. Since the British withdrawal from East of Suez, however, increased Soviet activity and an economic boom on Australia's west coast have led Australia to reorient its defense posture toward the Indian Ocean area. Despite the recent resignation of Prime Minister Gorton, indications seem to point toward a continuation of an internationalistic outlook on the part of the government rather than the resurgence of isolationism.

The Chinese Communists continue to pursue a cautious foreign policy, while building advanced strategic capabilities. In the wake of the "cultural revolution," a more practical approach to foreign affairs—articulated by Chou En-lai—may be discerned. The Chinese have attempted to ameliorate their disputes and improve their relations with the Soviet Union, although the basic problems remain. They give no indication of direct intervention in Indochina unless North Vietnam is invaded. Most significantly, Peking has responded cautiously to overtures from the United States, most notably, in permitting the much publicized visit of the American table tennis team to China in early April 1971. Changes in Sino-American relations could have important implications both for Peking and the United States, especially in their diplomacy with the Soviet Union. If, for example, the rivalry between China and the Soviet Union is irreparable, it might serve the interests of Moscow and Peking, respectively, to achieve a settlement of the Vietnam war in which neither China nor the Soviet Union enjoys a paramount position. Such a contingency might also serve U.S. interests.

Yet the Sino-Soviet dispute, though undoubtedly of great significance, remains particularly difficult to analyze. In Southeast Asia, the Soviet Union cannot be displeased by a war which costs the United States extraordinary treasure and political demoralization and, at the same time, increases the difficulty of a rapprochement between the United States and China. It is well worth the billion dollars in Soviet economic and military supplies annually supplied to North Vietnam. The Soviet Union can take much of the credit for whatever success North Vietnam has enjoyed in the war. Meanwhile, it can put political and military "teeth" into its version of an Asian security sphere by preparing "means of containment" against the Chinese.

The foregoing analysis suggests that, like the British withdrawal from East of Suez, the United States withdrawal from Vietnam will create political power vacuums—if only perceived by observant statesmen. The Soviet Union could, either alone or with the assistance of others, fill the vacuum for three different reasons:

(1) The containment of China being paramount, the Soviet Union presents itself as the alternative to the United States in protecting Southeast Asia and the Pacific from China. The tangible evidence is the presence of the Soviet Navy, as well as increased Soviet influence in the Persian Gulf (which is the source of Japan's oil). But the major evidence of the power of the Soviet Union is the development of nuclear armaments capable of deterring both the United States and Communist China. The Soviet Union would make an effort to enlist Japan, India, and Indonesia in restraint of the Chinese. Thus, the greater the appearance of a U.S. defeat in Vietnam, the better would be the Soviet opportunity to present its power as a substitute.

(2) Widespread recognition that the Soviet Union had become the dominant superpower would erode the U.S. security system. In this scenario, the Soviet Union would compete for influence with both Communist China and the United States while assiduously avoiding any military commitment. Thus, what must be avoided by the Soviet Union during the process of American withdrawal is the creation of Soviet security commitments to unreliable local states.

(3) The Soviet Union would work tacitly toward preserving U.S. security arrangements in the offshore island chain (Japan, Taiwan and the Philippines) since it would prefer that China also face a potential two-front struggle—the USSR alone cannot be the sole bulwark against China. The Soviet Union might regard Japanese rearmament as not really controllable and a Soviet-Japanese alliance as unlikely. Even more unlikely is any real rapprochement between the Soviet Union and the Republic of China on Taiwan. Under these circumstances, paradoxically, the retention by Japan and Taiwan of their security links with the United States would serve Soviet interests. If the Soviet Union adopts this condominium policy, the Vietnam war—from its point of view—should be concluded swiftly but without a stunning defeat for the U.S. Prolonging the war might work to China's advantage.

45

Western Hemisphere: U.S.-Canadian Relations

The major problem areas are: (1) Canada's loss of a sense of destiny as a "middle power" in world affairs; (2) Canadian sensitivity about the dominant position of U.S. investments in Canada; and (3) the Quebec separatist issue.

For much of the generation after World War II, the Canadians conceived of their international mission as the anticipation and mediation of U.S. activities in world affairs. Recently, Canada has suffered three reverses nearly fatal to this sense of mission. On the eve of the Six-Day War of June 1967, the Canadians were forced to withdraw their peacekeeping force from Egypt, in marked contrast to the 1956 Suez crisis when Foreign Minister Lester Pearson took an active diplomatic initiative. Canada has played little part in the Middle East crisis since 1967. Moreover, its relationship with India was damaged when Canada joined with India in the International Control Commission in Southeast Asia and found the experience to be an unhappy one. Finally, the Canadian government was chagrined when France, although an ally, actively interfered to encourage Quebec's separatism through General de Gaulle's visit and other maneuvers. Even the U.S. proposals of the early 1960s for an Atlantic partnership did not accord fully with Canadian interests. The U.S. endorsement of the "dumbbell" theory, which posits a partnership between the United States-Canada and Europe, would either have left Canada in limbo or drawn her closer to the United States. Canadian policy is designed to enable Canada to live in harmony with, but independent of, the United States.

The decline in Canadian interest in European affairs is matched by recognition of Communist China and growing economic ties with Japan—which appear to Canadians as counterweights to U.S. investments. In addition to these troubles, U.S.-Canadian relations have been strained by disagreement over the Vietnam war, and the flight to Canada of Americans avoiding the draft.

Fundamental shifts in Canada's foreign policy are accompanied by pressing internal problems. There is growing hostility to U.S. investment despite the recognition of its vital importance for Canadian economic development. United States investment in Canada, currently at a level of about $35 billion is greater than the U.S. investment in any other country or region of the world. It amounts to a third of all United States foreign investment worldwide, and is larger than all our investments in the European Common Market plus Great Britain and larger than those in Asia and Africa combined. It encompasses some 97 percent of the automobile and petroleum industries of Canada, 46 percent of all manufacturing, and some 50 percent of Canada's economy. This huge investment has led many Canadian nationalists to complain of an American "take-over"—which might also be reversed to say "sellout." It is now a very sensitive issue in Canada and will shortly result in the completion of a government White Paper on investment. This in turn may bring about new legislation imposing controls and restrictions in as yet unknown directions.

Few Canadians realize that Canadian citizens, for their part, have private investment in the United States amounting to $6 billion. A distinction between these two investments is that the U.S. investment in Canada is almost all direct whereas the Canadian investment in the United States is primarily portfolio. On a per capita basis, however, Canadian investment in the United States is almost twice as great as the U.S. investment in Canada.

Moreover, there is the issue of Quebec "separation," which has generated violence in French Canada and could provide fertile soil for a "war of national liberation" in the heart of the North American continent. There is as yet no direct evidence that communist powers or agents have been meddling in the Quebec separatist movement or have aggravated it. If the movement makes further advances, it will of course provide an incentive for such intervention and meddling, as has occurred in many other parts of the world. But the chief problem here is that if Quebec should separate from Canada for reasons which are basically much more psychological and emotional than economic or political, then what will happen to the Maritime Provinces and to British Columbia? And if such political instability occurs in Canada, what will happen to the immense United States investment described above? And to our access to needed raw materials? It is clear that, if Quebec does separate, it would not wish to join the United States. The same would hold true for the Maritimes and British Columbia.

Western Hemisphere: Latin America and the Caribbean

The severe economic, social and political problems of Latin America, continued deterioration of U.S.-Latin American relations and greater Soviet activity in the region suggest that Latin America will become an important arena for Soviet operations in the seventies.

The Alliance for Progress, born one decade ago, was heralded as a ten-year panacea for the centuries-old instability, poverty and injustice which have plagued most of Latin America. But the impact of the tremendous population explosion was not correctly assessed, and economic growth in many Latin American countries was more than offset by the millions of new mouths to feed. Political instability is endemic. There have been more than 20 coups d'etat in twelve countries in Latin America in the last eight years. The Alliance for Progress, launched with such high promise, has failed to achieve its objectives. The unfulfilled hopes it raised in Latin America have engendered only frustration and anti-Americanism.

U.S.-Latin American relations are worsening. Nationalism and accompanying anti-Americanism have become increasingly virulent in many Latin American countries, and black power movements, which are basically anti-American, have become strident forces of political ferment in several Caribbean states. Anti-American leftist, "Nasserite" military juntas now hold power in Peru and Bolivia. U.S. relations with Panama and Ecuador are strained over the issues of land and ocean sovereignty, respectively. Uruguay has a serious urban guerrilla problem. The Soviet Union has concluded negotiations for establishing an embassy in Costa

Rica (the "model" democratic nation in Central America), and has signed trade agreements exchanging millions of dollars worth of Costa Rican coffee for Soviet agricultural machinery. Throughout the continent the influx of population into cities—a phenomenon common throughout Latin America—creates a vast group whose problems and frustrations may be exploited by urban guerrilla insurgents in the next decade. Diplomatic kidnapping aimed solely at U.S. and European diplomats is much in vogue currently.

Moreover, the election of an avowed Marxist, Salvadore Allende, as President of a coalition government in Chile can only bode ill for U.S.-Chilean relations. Allende has established diplomatic relations with Cuba, thus breaching the explicit agreement of the Organization of American States (OAS). Economic links between Cuba and Chile are being strengthened. Allende may move to a one-party system or he may prefer to retain power through a leftist coalition as economic difficulties beset the nationalization projects. Meanwhile, preparations are being made for the Soviet fishing fleet to use the Chilean port of Valparaiso—a step which may foreshadow Soviet naval visits.

Brazil, the largest country in Latin America, is currently governed by a military regime which has thus far managed to restrain a well organized communist underground. Brazil, which faced the threat of a communist take-over during the presidency of Goulart, might yet move in that direction. While the United States is almost compelled to adopt a "low profile" approach, the Soviet Union has succeeded in raising its "profile" and influence in the area.

In the last ten years the USSR has considerably increased its political and economic leverage over Cuba. It has established naval facilities capable of servicing a Caribbean flotilla at Cienfuegos, and it probably operates both conventional and nuclear-powered submarines from submarine tenders there. It also has the capability to operate nuclear missile-armed submarines from Cienfuegos but there is no evidence that this has yet been done. Since July 1969, the Soviet naval colors have been shown near the shores of a host of Caribbean countries by three different Soviet task forces. Cuba is important to the Soviet Union as a base for intelligence gathering and a training ground for political warfare operations in the Caribbean and South America.

Soviet use of the Cienfuegos base has direct strategic consequences. Submarine tending facilities there reduce the time normally spent in traveling to and from Soviet firing stations off our Atlantic and Gulf coasts. Indeed, missiles from Soviet nuclear submarines could reach some U.S. targets while such craft were still moored in the Cienfuegos harbor.

The mere presence of a Soviet task force in the Caribbean serves to reduce U.S. freedom of movement in dealing with the recurring political crises in the areas. Clearly, the U.S. responses to the Cuban missile crisis of 1962 and the Dominican Republic crisis of 1965 depended to a significant degree upon U.S. military superiority in that strategic sea. The presence of a Soviet task force in the Caribbean area at those times would, at the very least, have complicated both operations. If the Soviet naval presence does become permanent, which is likely, the effects may be far-reaching. The Caribbean is no longer an "American lake."

The Soviet naval presence in the Caribbean represents one of the fruits of the Soviet naval buildup of the past decade. The lengthening shadow of Soviet naval power is a result of a vast investment in military technology. A Soviet naval capability in close proximity to the United States complicates not only the defense of the United States, but in an age of strategic parity renders the fulfillment of U.S. commitments in other regions in the world more difficult.

The Cuban bridgehead in Latin America gives the Soviet Union the opportunity, on the one hand, to pursue its objectives by conventional diplomacy and by encouraging orthodox communist parties to follow the *via pacifica* to power; and, on the other hand, to give direct support to guerrilla movements throughout Latin America, or to permit Cuba to encourage, finance, and arm them. Occasionally, such activities boomerang, as exemplified by the March 1971 discovery in Mexico of clandestine guerrillas who had attended Patrice Lumumba University in Moscow and were trained in North Korea. Nonetheless, by being able to walk both the "straight" and devious sides of the street, the Soviet Union can achieve a flexibility in the seventies which it did not enjoy throughout the sixties. The USSR begins this decade with the backlash from the demonstrated American failure to improve the lot of Latin America in the sixties. U.S. prestige, already low, appears to be diminishing even further as it becomes apparent that the United States is unwilling (or unable) to prevent the Soviet Navy from assuming a role as a major force in the area. While American conventional power in this hemisphere exceeds Soviet forces by far, the strengthened Soviet strategic position probably ensures that there will never be a repetition of the 1962 Cuban missile crisis scenario in which the United States, because of its overwhelming strategic superiority, forced the Soviet Union to withdraw its missiles from Cuba.

Many Latin American governments have shown increasing interest in improved relations with the Soviet Union. To some extent this interest has been sparked by growing U.S. indifference, isolationism, and protectionism. The Soviet Union is moving swiftly to exploit these new opportunities for expanding its bridgehead in the New World. Today one can see a loose bloc of new, highly nationalistic revolutionary governments emerging in Latin America. The political affinities of such centralized "Nasserite" governments as those in Peru and Bolivia are clear. Whether or not those governments, together with Chile and Cuba, form the embryo of a "socialist" bloc and a new sphere of Soviet influence remains to be seen.

The total of the many small incremental diplomatic, political and economic gains that the Soviet Union has made in Latin America in the last decade is impressive. Furthermore, the incrementalist approach which the Soviet Union has utilized since 1962 has been pursued so quietly that the United States, undisturbed by violent shock, hews to a policy of "benign neglect." In view of the continued deterioration of U.S.-Latin American relations in general, the Soviet Union probably correctly anticipates that the incrementalist approach will continue to garner small but, in sum, significant gains.

A Soviet policy of:

(1) *opportunity* would make Latin America an increasingly important area in which to demonstrate Soviet nuclear and conventional strength, by seeking to constrain American ability to prevent action against U.S. interests in a region close to the United States;

(2) *caution* would entail continuation of the incrementalist trend of the past decade without recourse to overt military power save in the unlikely circumstance of an invasion of Cuba by U.S.-supported forces; and

(3) *condominium* would attempt the diplomatic demarcation of spheres of influence, with the Soviet Union agreeing to desist from further inroads into Latin America in return for American acceptance of Soviet hegemony in the Middle East and the Eastern Mediterranean.

Conclusion

The foregoing regional "tour" reveals the flexibility of Soviet foreign policy. There seems to be a relationship, however, between the emphasis of this policy—opportunity, caution, condominium—and the strategic or conventional forces available. As has been shown, especially in the Middle East, the Soviet Union is adept at manipulating its growing local strength and its strategic arsenal for great political advantage. The decline in the effectiveness of the American strategic umbrella enables the Soviet Union to deploy its conventional military capacity more aggressively. The conclusion is inescapable that the growth of Soviet military power is being accompanied by the spread of the "opportunity" emphasis in Soviet foreign policy.